D0195293

BETWEEN PEOPLE

also by John A. Sanford
published by Paulist Press

HEALING AND WHOLENESS
DREAMS AND HEALING
THE INVISIBLE PARTNERS
THE KINGDOM WITHIN
THE MAN WHO WRESTLED WITH GOD

BETWEEN PEOPLE

Communicating One-to-One

John A. Sanford

PAULIST PRESS
New York/Ramsey

Acknowledgments:
My great gratitude to Helen Macey
whose help in preparing this manuscript
has been, as always, invaluable.
And my special thanks to my wife,
Linny, who contributed many ideas and suggestions
to this book, and has helped me to learn many things
about communication through the years.

Library of Congress
Catalog Card Number: 81–84350

ISBN: 0–8091–2440–8

Published by Paulist Press
545 Island Road, Ramsey, N.J. 07446

Printed and bound in the
United States of America

Contents

Chapter One
Communication and Relationship   1

Chapter Two
Working Through the Agenda   12

Chapter Three
The Power of Creative Listening   17

Chapter Four
Our Gigantic Emotions   31

Chapter Five
The Anima/Animus Fight   40

Chapter Six
The Proteus Problem   47

Chapter Seven
Guilt and Communication   60

Contents

Chapter Eight
Indirect Communication   73

Chapter Nine
People *Are* Different   84

*Dedicated to
all the persons
who have counseled
with me over the years
and taught me so much.*

A Note to the Reader

There are many kinds of communication. We speak of radio or newspapers or public programs as forms of communication. But this book is about interpersonal communication—communication between two people who have, or want to have, a relationship. Sometimes I will use the term "interpersonal communication," but at all times, whether I use that term or not, it is this kind of communication to which I am referring, unless otherwise specified.

Nowadays when you write a book you face the problem of which pronoun to use when indicating an indefinite person. If you say "When *he* wants to communicate he might try . . ." this seems to leave out members of the feminine sex. However, if you say "When he or she wants to communicate he or she might try . . ." this is awkward English. One solution is to be boldly chauvinistic and just use "he." The other is to try to be fair to everyone and wind up bending the English language into pretzels. I have opted for still another solution. Sometimes, when speaking of an indefinite person, I will refer to "he" and sometimes to "she." I haven't totaled the number of times I have used the masculine pronoun and how many times the feminine one, but I think the balance is about even. I hope this will satisfy as many readers as possible without being too hard on the written language.

Chapter One
Communication and Relationship

How marvelous is a ball! Its roundness endows it with unusual properties that are almost impossible to resist. Imagine that you are walking through the park and children are playing nearby with a ball. As you pass by the ball gets away from them and rolls toward you. Of course you will reach for it, eager as a child to catch it, challenged by the opportunity to throw it back to the players. And as you toss the ball back to the expectant children, for a moment you are connected with them. An appreciative shout and wave goes up from the children at your good and helpful toss of the ball, and with a friendly wave in return you are on your way again, your soul a bit richer because of the encounter with the magical ball, and your spirit momentarily energized by the playful exchange with the children that the ball made possible for you.

Communication between two people is like this because it is like tossing a ball back and forth. And just as in a game of catch both participants are energized and related to each other, so in effective communication energy flows, and two persons are linked together by the energy that goes back and forth between them.

1

People who play catch need each other; you cannot play catch by yourself. Communication also requires two people who are willing to play. And when they play, when the ball of communication goes back and forth between them, they are brought into relationship.

So interpersonal communication can be understood as a particular aspect of relationship, even as a necessity for relationship. We can think of relationship as something larger than communication; communication is contained in the idea of relationship, but is only a part of it, for relationship involves many things. Yet without communication, relationship would be impossible. Communication is like a bridge connecting two sides of a river; it is a span that links two people together and makes relationship possible. Without communication we would all be islands, separated from other islands by an unbridgeable body of water.

Communication is not the same as agreement between people. In fact, communication enables people to relate when they do *not* agree. People *are* different. They inevitably view life differently and often will not agree with each other. But relationship does not mean making people the same, or even insisting that they agree. The miracle of relationship is that it can connect people together in a positive, meaningful way who are different and so have a different view about things. Eros (personal warmth and caring) can bind people together who see things quite differently, but this connection is only possible when communication between them takes place.

Some people do not try to communicate with the important people in their lives because, they say mistakenly, "But when we talk, nothing ever gets worked out." By this they usually mean that no agreement has been reached on certain issues. Now this may be the case, but if the communication between them has been effective, this does not mean that nothing has happened. For where communication has worked, where the ball has been thrown and caught and tossed back again, something has changed. People are then connected together even though they do not agree.

It may help in describing communication to point out what it is not. Interpersonal communication is not lecturing. Lecturing can be regarded as a form of communication in general, and a perfectly legitimate one for certain purposes, such as the transmission of information or ideas. But lecturing is not interpersonal communication because it is one-sided, since the one who is doing the lecturing is doing all the talking. If interpersonal communication is like a game of catch, with a ball being tossed back and forth, lecturing is like one person throwing a series of balls toward others. It has its place in life, but it is not the form of communication that we are discussing in this book. Yet in many relationships people mistake lecturing for interpersonal communication. When someone has made a mistake, or done something we did not like, we say, "Well, I told him so!" Maybe we did, but the chances are it was a lecture, not communication.

Parents are especially prone to lecture their children rather than communicate with them. The effectiveness of such parental lectures dissipates quickly. As soon as the parent's lecture begins, the child is apt to put up a barrier. The words are spoken and heard, but the message is resisted. This is especially likely to be the case if the lecture has become familiar to the child. It usually has. Parents have a tendency to repeat the same lectures. It is as though the lectures are numbered, so the child says, "Well, here comes lecture number 22 again." Then the wall goes up, and no matter how full of parental wisdom the lecture might be, it has no effect.

The child resists the parent's lecture because she knows, somewhere in herself, that the parent is lecturing because it is easier to do this than to undertake the task of communication. As parents, when we lecture we think we have done our job. We do not realize that many times we have simply avoided the more difficult but more rewarding and helpful task of communicating with our child. The child then knows that her opinion and her feelings in the matter are not wanted. She feels diminished and unimportant, sometimes even unloved. Small wonder then that though she hears the parent's words she does not take them into her heart. It is as though one person throws a ball toward another, but the other person is distrustful and refuses to catch it because she thinks, "He doesn't really want to play catch with me; he only wants to throw the ball at me and have me run for it."

If interpersonal communication is not lecturing, neither does it consist in making pronouncements. Pronouncements are statements made by a person who assumes such an air of authority that others immediately comprehend that the matter is not open to discussion. We can usually tell when someone is lecturing us, but pronouncements are sometimes more subtle because the person making them may think he is trying to communicate. Sometimes people make pronouncements without even realizing what they are doing. Often the pronouncement lies in the tone of voice, not in the actual words that are said. But the other person is turned away by pronouncements; he gets the clear feeling that his thoughts in the matter are not going to be heard.

If communication is like a game of catch, a person who makes a pronouncement is like someone who throws a ball at another person and then walks away. What can the other person do? Even if he has caught the ball he is left standing there helplessly, for the other person does not want to play, he only wants to throw.

Pronouncements, like lectures, have their place in life. There are times when we need to do exactly this. When we want to "lay down the law" and say, "Now this is the way it is," we have to make pronouncements. The marine sergeant may not want to take up time communicating with the recruits. It is enough for him to make pronouncements, and then that is the way things will be. But pronouncements do not belong to the world of interpersonal communication, for the latter can take place only when the people involved are willing to receive the ball as well as to throw it.

But this does not stop people from making pronouncements, and people in positions of authority, like our marine sergeant, are especially prone to do this. Ministers, teachers, therapists, coaches, doctors, and parents are apt to be especially fond of making pronouncements, for since they are in positions of authority, it is tempting for them to assume an air of superiority when they speak. It is often easier, or so it seems, to try to settle a relationship matter by making pronouncements rather than by communication, for then there is no obligation to listen to the other person. When we expect or want the other person to be in a subservient or childlike relationship to us, pronouncements may be the order of the day. But if we want a mature response from a person, and a relationship of some equality, making pronouncements will not do, for the other person inevitably feels shut out, relegated to a childlike role. Very often that person's response to the pronouncement will, in fact, be something childlike: either a childish acquiescence, or a childish rebellion.

In a situation that calls for interpersonal communication, if we lecture instead, we are likely to arouse indifference or even derision in the other person. If we make pronouncements, we are likely to engender resentment and some kind of rebellious behavior intended to upset the air of authority we have assumed for ourselves. But we will probably never know the ill effects we have caused because the other person, sensing that no interchange is going to be possible, usually keeps his feelings to himself.

This brings up one of the many reasons why interpersonal communication is so important, for the opposite of communication is isolation, and isolation is the breeding ground for evil. C. G. Jung once said that the principle of evil was so strong that only two things could keep a person from either being its victim or its perpetrator: first, if a person's soul was filled with a spirit stronger than the spirit of evil; second, if a person was connected to other people in a warm, human community.

The latter can only come about where there has been communication among people. Without that communication people become isolated, and in that isolation evil can take root. Some people react to the evil of isolation by collapsing under it and gradually becoming ill in body or mind. Other people become actively taken over by evil and visit evil upon others. For instance, when we examine the lives of those cold-blooded killers in our society who wantonly and without apparent motivation kill others, we inevitably find persons who have been emotionally isolated. Unable to communicate with their fellow human beings they eventually turn against them.

For communication to take place it has to start in the right way. In a game of catch, the ball must be thrown in such a way that it can be caught by the other person so she can toss it back to us. It is important when playing catch that the first toss be a good one, that the ball be thrown within reach of the other player, resolutely enough to reach her, but gently enough so she can handle it. If two people are playing catch and one person throws the ball wildly so the other has to keep chasing it, the game will soon break up. Or if one person throws as hard as he can at the other person's head, the other person may become angry and refuse to play any longer.

We know this about playing catch, but we forget it when we start to communicate, for many of us make an opening toss that is bound to have negative results.

Joan says to Bill, "You don't care about me, but only about yourself. You are selfish, like your father."

This is like aiming the opening toss of the ball at the other person's head. Of course, it is probably better than saying nothing, for it *is* a reaching out for communication, an opening move to start something going. But it is not the most helpful way to start communication because Bill, in our hypothetical situation, can hardly help but have a negative reaction toward Joan's opening statement. Chances are Bill will either avoid discussion altogether (for instance, by leaving the house), or make a counter-accusation. In terms of our image of the game, Bill responds to Joan's hard opening toss of the ball either by refusing to play, or by picking up the ball and angrily hurling it back at her as hard as she hurled it at him.

Or perhaps it is Bill who has something on his mind. Tartly he says, "This is the tenth time I have asked you to stop at the camera shop on your way home from your office and pick up the camera I left to be fixed. I do things for you, but you are always forgetting the things I ask you to do for me because you only think of yourself."

The word "always" is usually a sure sign that the opening toss is going to be a wild one. When we use this word, it brings up such a sweeping generalization that discussion is almost impossible.

But what if Bill and Joan did do the things of which they are accused? What if they are guilty of the accusations made against them?

That may be the case, and if what we want to do is make the other person feel guilty, perhaps to get back at them, then the thing to do is to start out with an accusation. But if we want to communicate we need to know that this is not a helpful opening remark, for the fact is that most people have a difficult time handling guilt. We do not like to feel guilty, and we do not like people who make us feel guilty; most of us have weak egos that cannot accept a lot of guilt thrown at us. The result is that an opening remark that engenders guilt in the other person is almost certain to evoke a defensive or hostile reaction.

So starting effective communication requires giving some thought to the opening remark, since the way the dialogue starts often determines the way it will go. One helpful way of starting communication is to begin with an expression of our feeling, instead of with an accusatory statement.

To go back to our examples: Instead of accusing Bill outright of being selfish, Joan could have said to him, "I felt alone at the party last night. It made me angry when you seemed to want to be with your friends more than with me."

And Bill might have said to Joan "I was annoyed last night when I came home and found you had not run that errand for me. It made me feel that I am not important to you."

Of course there still is a note of accusation in these opening statements. There is no way to get around the fact that Joan is critical of Bill, and Bill of Joan. Nevertheless, an opening statement that expresses a person's feeling is more likely to receive a positive and helpful response than an opening statement that engenders guilt.

Another way of opening communication is with a statement of *our* problem. For instance, Bill might have said, "You know, I have a problem. Whenever you forget to run an errand for me I feel that you are forgetting because you don't care about me." Actually, such a statement may be true. It may be mostly Bill's problem that he magnifies small incidents into large ones.

Or Joan might have said, "You know, I have a problem at these parties, because when you go off with your friends I don't seem to know how to handle myself." And maybe Joan does have a problem. Should Bill stand by the side of his wife so she will not feel left out? Can she not circulate and talk to people on her own? All of this, of course, is what the two people must work out together. Maybe communication will help both of them to learn something about themselves.

To use another hypothetical example: Harry is upset because his wife, Susan, is drinking again. One evening he says sarcastically, "Well, I guess this is the way it's going to be now, just one drunken evening after another." Of course his wife erupts angrily.

Later, after thinking about it, he brings the subject up again. This time he begins by saying, "Susan, I have to tell you that when you drink I feel it destroys our relationship. That's why I wish you would stop."

Susan is angry again, but her anger does not last long this time. And she stops drinking, for now she knows how her husband feels and that what he values is the relationship, where before she felt he was just hostile and critical toward her.

If what we want to do is to communicate, we must remember that it is not enough to be right. Communication is not a matter of being right, but of starting a flow of energy between two people that can result in mutual understanding. If this is what we want, we must take the human reality of the other person into consideration and not throw more at her than she can handle.

Actually, taking the other person into consideration is essential for all forms of communication. For instance, an effective lecturer not only has his ideas well in mind, he also is observing his audience, watching them and sensing whether or not his ideas are reaching them. As an author writes her book she has in mind the kind of people she expects will read it and presents her material accordingly; if she does not do this, she is likely to wind up writing only to herself. Indeed, the rule of effective writing is, "Never forget your reader."

If this is true with lecturing or writing, it is even more true with interpersonal communication: the people we are trying to reach must be taken into account. It is helpful if we say things so they will be able to receive them.

Only when people communicate do they know each other. We can live with people for years and still be strangers when there is no communication. Young people especially sometimes say, "My parents don't even know who I am. They don't ever listen to me, so they don't know what I am thinking or feeling. They think they know me, but I am really a stranger to them."

Many years ago I ran across a letter from a young woman to a magazine describing how it felt to her when her parents did not listen to her. This letter is the inspiration for the following imaginary letter which such a young woman might write if she felt that during her childhood she had not been heard:

"I know I love my parents, and that they love me, but they have spoiled my life because they do not listen. Whenever I tried to talk with them they always said, 'Later ... I can't talk now ... I'm too busy.' When they did listen they often said to me, 'That's stupid to feel that way about it ...' Or, 'I know. I went through the same thing myself.' But I know they hadn't gone through the same thing, and that they didn't know how I felt.

When they said things like that, or would not listen, then I stopped trying to talk with them at all. It made me feel there was no point in talking to them, and it hurt so much when they misunderstood me or would not pay attention.

My parents showed their love for me by being responsible. They didn't want me to do anything wrong because this would show they had done something wrong and then God would punish us all. So they sent me to a religious boarding school. They made me go so I would not turn out wrong. They always tried to keep me from doing what was wrong instead of listening to me so I could figure things out for myself.

So where am I now? I drink too much, take drugs, and have had lots of sex with boys but no love. I am terribly confused.

The worst thing is that if my parents read this letter they would have no idea who wrote it. That is why if I had

one thing to say to parents it would be; Stop talking for a
while and listen, listen, listen."

Our imaginary young woman has admonished parents to
listen, listen, and listen again. It is essential for *all* persons who
want to communicate to listen, not only parents. In a future
chapter we will look at what goes into the process of creative
listening, but first we need to examine more closely what happens in communication once the opening toss has been made and
caught and the process has started.

Chapter Two
Working Through the Agenda

An agenda is a list of things we want to accomplish or work through. For instance, in a business meeting the agenda includes the different items that must be brought up for discussion and settlement. When two people are living together they inevitably accumulate an agenda of issues that need to be brought up, discussed and resolved. Sometimes the agenda goes back a long time and includes items that one person may have forgotten long ago, but the other person has kept alive. Or the agenda may include only what happened yesterday, or some plans for the future. Frequently the agenda includes many different items, but there is usually one that is of uppermost importance.

Communication is a matter of working through the agenda, and its success depends on the ability of those involved to work through the agendas of both. But this is not as easy as it sounds because many times one person blocks the other person's agenda. At other times the agenda is only partially worked through; some things have been discussed but the most important items have not been brought up yet.

To use our image of communication as a game of catch: When one person throws the ball it is an attempt to begin to work through an agenda with the other person. If the other person will not catch the ball and toss it back, the whole process is aborted. And if the ball is not thrown back and forth long enough, all the items of the agenda are not discussed.

If someone has something important to discuss, you might think he would bring it up right away, that the opening toss of the ball would have to do with the most important matter to be discussed. Very often this is the case, but not always. Sometimes a person brings up something of lesser importance to see if the atmosphere is correct for discussion before risking bringing up more difficult matters. At other times a person may not even know what his agenda is. We often begin a discussion under the impetus of a vaguely defined but powerful emotion. There is something we want to communicate, but we do not know what it is, and we will not know until the flow of communication has started and our emotions bring the deeper matters to the surface.

For instance, John may come home and begin to complain about things around the house. Mary, his wife, cannot see that things are all that bad and, wisely, begins to suspect that something else is really the matter. Because she listens long enough, and doesn't get hurt or defensive, she eventually finds out about the things that went wrong at the office. *That* is what John really wanted to talk about; *that* was the concern he had to communicate, but he hardly knew that himself until he began talking.

Or, John may be surprised when Mary starts to complain about the way he does not pick up his clothes and put them away. He can see her point and why this bothers her, but it strikes him that the amount of emotion she is showing is larger than the situation warrants. However he patiently discusses the matter with Mary, and as the discussion proceeds, she gets to her genuine concern: her anger at him because the day before, when she disciplined the children, he objected to her method in front of them. This made her feel unsupported and undermined, and she had to express her anger about this in order to be related to her husband again. The matter of John's leaving his clothes on the floor was important too because it was an annoyance to her and would bother her until it was worked out. But that was only one item on her agenda, and not the most important one.

A mother brings her son home from nursery school. He sees his playmates from his neighborhood outside their home and at first seems pleased, but then, unaccountably, says to them rudely, "Go away; you are not my friends!" The mother's first impulse is to scold her son, but she is perplexed by his hostile attitude and decides not to make an issue of it for the time being. Only later does she learn from the nursery school teacher that the other boys at the school have been excluding her son from their play, saying to him, "Go away with your dark skin; you are not one of us." The boy is too small to know how to tell his mother about his problem at school and how badly his feelings have been hurt. The only way he knows to communicate his pain is to inflict it on others, even though they have not hurt him. His behavior is an attempt to let others see his need. In this case it succeeded because the mother persisted in finding out what was wrong. She heard her son correctly—he was expressing pain—and did not let herself be distracted by his surface behavior.

As everyone knows who has been to a business meeting or a conference, it takes time to work through an agenda. That is why anything that blocks the flow of energy in discussion is disruptive to communication. One of the most frequent blocks is interruption. Interruption is disruptive to communication because it stops the other person's flow of energy. Moreover, when others interrupt us we feel as though we have not been heard; it is as though we were starting to throw the ball to them in our game of catch but they reached out and snatched it away from us. Then instead of throwing it back to us they ran away with it.

There are various reasons why we interrupt other people. One important reason is because we have our own agenda and can't wait to get to it; often something the other person has said reminds us of it. So without waiting for the other person to complete his throw we take the ball away to make our own toss. This is regrettable, but understandable and even forgivable if it does not happen too often. But sometimes we interrupt others for deeper reasons: We do not like what we are hearing, so we interrupt in order to change the course of the discussion. Interrupting is our way of defending ourselves against something that is unpleasant; it becomes one of the many avoidance techniques we will look at more closely in a later chapter.

However, occasionally we interrupt because the other person keeps on talking and talking and unless we interrupt we will never be heard. Worse yet, we might become dominated by the other person's talk which is no longer an attempt at communication, but a harangue that has the desire for control as its objective. Then we have to grab the ball from the other person by interrupting. Even then, if we must interrupt, it is best to do so by saying something such as: "But you aren't letting me say anything." If we simply barge in with what we want to say, the other person may in turn interrupt us, and the whole conversation, if it can be called that, breaks down. By pointing out to the other person that he is not letting us have our say we make an appeal to his better nature and it is possible for the talk to be on a more equal basis. Effective communication at this point calls for patience and maturity: the patience to listen to what the other person is saying before we interject our agenda, and the maturity to be able to indicate to the other person that we have heard him.

It is extremely important for us to know that the significant people in our lives have heard us. Even if they do not agree with us, we need to feel heard; otherwise we will think that all our attempts to communicate have failed. Not being heard produces frustration, isolation, and anger. If we are not heard the first time, we may try again, and once again, but if we feel the other person is refusing to hear us at all, we may give up.

The magic number is three. For some reason we will usually give another person three chances to hear us. If all three attempts to be heard and understood fail, the chances are that we will stop. "Three strikes and you are out." It is something every counselor finds out as he listens to his clients. They will give him three times to hear what they are saying, but if he fails after the third time the chances are they will clam up, and the counselor may never know why the interview suddenly went dead. But what happens in counseling is only a variant of what happens in any form of interpersonal communication.

It helps, then, to learn how to hear what the other person is saying, and how to let him know we have heard by making a proper response. True, we have our own agenda that may be bursting to come out, but it can wait. Listen first. Indicate in a reply that you have heard, and you will find that the other person is satisfied. He feels fulfilled in his attempt to be heard. A miracle has happened: Now *he* can hear *us*.

This is easy to say, but not so easy to do. It takes understanding and discipline to listen to other people creatively and hear what they are saying. That is what we will discuss in our next chapter.

Chapter Three

The Power of Creative Listening

Creative listening takes place when one person devotes her attention wholeheartedly to what another person is saying. Creative listening is receptive, but not passive. It is receptive because the listener is taking in what the other person is saying, feeling, and experiencing. It is active and not passive because the listener is actively seeking to understand what the other person is expressing.

There is healing power in creative listening because it develops a climate between two people in which relationship and understanding can grow. It also relieves isolation and, as we saw in a previous chapter, this tends to prevent evil from developing.

Because listening creatively is healing, psychotherapists develop their powers to hear what other people are saying. The annals of psychotherapy are full of stories in which the capacity of the therapist to listen creatively released the self-healing in a client and brought about a cure. A dramatic story of such a cure is found in Robert Lindner's book, *The Fifty Minute Hour*. In the last chapter of this book Dr. Lindner discusses a brilliant physicist who became psychotic. In the physicist's psychosis he developed an elaborate science fiction fantasy that was so real to

17

him that he lived within it to the exclusion of what is ordinarily called reality. Dr. Lindner decided to listen carefully to his patient as he told him of his fantasies of space and planets and interstellar travel. It soon became quite absorbing for the doctor as well as the patient, and as the weeks went by Lindner tells us that he became more and more involved. He began to anticipate the hour with his client so he could hear about further developments in this great fantasy world; in short, he was listening attentively. But eventually Dr. Lindner noticed a difference in his patient. Even though the physicist told his stories as usual, something was not the same. Gradually Lindner realized the physicist no longer believed in what he was saying. Confronted with this the patient admitted that for some time he had realized that what he was telling was fantasy and not real fact. In other words, he was no longer psychotic. Why had he not told the doctor this before? The reply was that Lindner had become so interested he did not want to disappoint him.

Here is an example of a therapist who helped his client by creative listening. Lindner never interpreted the meaning of the fantasies, never delved into the physicist's past or used any of the procedures many Freudian or Jungian analysts would have employed. But by listening he got inside of his patient's fantasy world and this cured him, for there is room for only one person in a psychosis. Once the isolation of the physicist was broken by Lindner's creative listening, the man came out of his psychotic state.

This is an example of the power of creative listening, but it must not be supposed that such listening is a technique that is reserved for the use of psychotherapists. Creative listening is a fundamental and important part of all human relationships. It is essential for all of us to learn to listen creatively to others: friends listen to friends, employers to their employees and vice versa, parents to children, husbands and wives to each other. We even need to learn to listen to our enemies and those who oppose us in life. In this way we may turn a hostile relationship around, or, at least, learn something important.

There are many reasons why so many people lack the art of creative listening in our culture. First, because creative listening does not come naturally but is, for most people, a skill that must be acquired. We would like to think that the capacity to relate comes naturally, but to a great extent it is something that must be learned in life just as other abilities must be learned. It is something that requires work.

Second, many people lack the art of creative listening because of what it is not. It is not lecturing. It is not giving advice. It is not admonishing someone. It is not making pronouncements. It is not judging. All of these functions, as we noted earlier, may have their place in human communication, but they do not belong in creative listening. When we want to listen we must be careful to rule out that part of us that wants to lecture, admonish, advise or judge. But right here is where many people fail at listening, for the judging-lecturing-advising side of us wants to jump in and take over. To listen effectively we must be able to put aside these other functions, at least for the time being. This means that when we listen to someone we must reject the temptation to leap in and say, "Let me tell you what I would do . . ." or "I understand exactly what you are feeling . . ."

Listening creatively, and not jumping in with our advice, helps a person work through her agenda. We have already noted that when people want to communicate they have, as a rule, an agenda they must work through. When we listen it gives them the opportunity to work through all of their agenda. It gives them the satisfaction of having been able to express all of the things that were bothering them, all those matters and feelings that wanted to be shared.

But here we run into a problem, for the chances are that we have our agenda too. Especially in a close interpersonal relationship, both persons have their agendas, and when people start to talk with us about their feelings we naturally want to bring up our feelings as well. Nevertheless, if we wish to listen creatively we must learn to put aside our own agenda for the time being and listen to what the other person is saying. Perhaps the other person will then listen to us as well. If not, the relationship will become unequal and will lose its staying power, for to keep a relationship going both people must put energy into it. First we honor the other person's need to express himself, if he has been the one to begin the dialogue; then we should have our turn.

When our turn comes, and we have listened to the other person and heard what he is saying, we will find that our agenda is more likely to be heard than would have been possible if we had not listened first. For, as noted before, when someone tries to express himself to another person, and that person refuses to listen, the first person feels frustrated and blocked and is not in a position to hear what is being said back. But if a person feels he has been heard, he is open to hearing someone else.

This is why I said that certain skills in relationship do not come naturally, for it takes discipline on our part to hear what another person is saying, and to listen until he is through. It takes discipline to hold back our own list of grievances or whatever else is on our mind. We can think of this devotion to listening as a sacrifice, for we sacrifice our own agenda for the time being, and devote our energy in a sacrificial way to the other person. This requires and develops maturity, for it takes maturity to be able to sacrifice in this way for the sake of communication.

Truly it has been said that we become what we do. Listening is a maturing activity. If we listen creatively it will not only help the other person, it will also help us to mature.

Creative listening is simple, but it is also hard work. It is like cutting down a tree with an axe. There are only a few basic principles to follow when cutting down a tree, but it is hard work. And listening is hard work, for it requires a concentration of energy on another person and what he is saying and feeling. In fact, it is usually more important to hear feelings than content.

Once we have heard what another person is saying it often helps to reflect that back to him. Let us take the situation in which a man has come home from work and has begun to complain about things around the house. His wife might say, "It sounds as if you are angry at me." This gives her husband a chance to clarify the situation. He might answer, "No, I am not angry at you. I am angry, but it is not at you, but at what happened at the office today." In this way a potentially serious misunderstanding can be resolved. Also, when we reflect back what we have heard the other person say, we are indicating to him that we have truly heard him. In terms of our analogy, we have shown him that we have seen and caught the ball, and are ready to play the game with him.

Simple, but hard work. That is creative listening. And precisely because it *is* hard work we do not listen to everyone, nor can we always be available to people who want us to listen to them. For instance, if a person has been drinking we may decline to listen to her. It does no good to listen to a person who is under the influence of alcohol; it drains us, without helping her. The situation is similar with regard to people under the influence of drugs. Sometimes it does not help people to listen to them on the telephone either (though not always). The reason for this is that when a person calls us on the phone it is at that person's convenience, but perhaps at our inconvenience. Many people call others and immediately start to talk out their agenda without inquiring if it is a good time for such a talk or not. This may reflect a manipulative or egocentric attitude on the part of that person, and if, through a false feeling of guilt, we feel compelled to listen to that person, we do not help her but only confirm her in her egocentric attitude.

In short, it does not do anyone any good to listen to another person unless that person is talking responsibly. To listen to someone is like giving him a gift. It does no good to give a gift unless we want to give it, or feel it is part of our integrity to give it. For instance, a counselor may listen to a client whether she wants to or not because the client is paying her to listen. Even if she is not in a mood to listen she is a professional who honors her obligation to her client and has carefully developed the ability to respond to a client's needs when called upon to do so at an appropriate time. A sensitive parent might also listen to a small child who has a sudden need to be heard, even though she might not want to listen at that moment. She listens when the child wants to be heard because she knows that the child's need is *now* and cannot be postponed; she wants to honor this in the child, and feels it is her appointed task to listen then if she possibly can. But this willingness to listen no matter how we feel at the time does not extend to everyone. In fact, even the counselor or parent might have to ask for a postponement of a listening situation if he or she is not able to do it at the time. There are times when we cannot listen to others because we do not have the energy; we may be fragmented, exhausted, or too absorbed with our own problems. In this case we might make an appointment at some definite future time to discuss the matter. This gives us the opportunity to become inwardly ready to listen and to have energy available for the other person.

One person's idea of what is the wrong time for discussing a matter may differ from another person's idea. Let us say it is 1:00 A.M. John is tired and is facing a hard day at the office in the morning, but Mary has something on her mind. Testily she begins to bring it up but John complains. It is late. He is tired. He has to work the next day. "Why do you bring that up now?" he says angrily. But Mary refuses to give up. All day John has been too busy to talk with her, and it was this way over the weekend too. "I am talking to you now because this is the only time when you can't run away," she retorts resentfully.

Who is right, John or Mary? Is Mary bringing up the difficult matter at 1:00 A.M. just to punish John for ignoring her? Or has he brought the difficulty on himself by turning his wife away so much that she has no other recourse than to try to talk to him now? One thing is certain—the timing Mary chose brings up a whole new matter to be discussed: How they are relating, or failing to relate. Whether John will get up and discuss the matter with her at 1:00 A.M. or whether Mary will agree to wait until morning will depend, of course, on how the couple chooses to deal with the situation.

As we have seen, creative listening often has helpful and unexpected results because it enables people to work through their agendas. For this reason, when creative listening occurs matters sometimes come up that no one could have anticipated. The following example illustrates this.

Some years ago I taught a class on counseling for older students who were training for the ministry. The main emphasis of the course was on creative listening and reflective (non-directive) counseling. To help the student-pastors acquire this skill they were asked to interview people in hospitals, or in some other crisis situation, and bring in a verbatim report of what transpired. One of my students was a patient in a hospital at this time, being treated for a minor ailment. His roommate was a rough fellow whom he called "Tiny" because of his great size. During the student-pastor's stay in the hospital a friend came to visit him, and Tiny could not help but overhear their conversation. From this Tiny learned that his roommate was a pastor. This led to the following conversation between Tiny and my student, who used it for his verbatim report. The portions in parentheses are my own comments on the replies the student made to Tiny's conversation.

Tiny (beginning the conversation): Are you a preacher or something?

Student-Pastor: Well, in a way—I have my own business, but I am going to school studying for the ministry.

Tiny: My wife and I went to our preacher but he sent us to a marriage counselor.

(Having satisfied himself that he is with a minister, who is someone he can talk to about his problems, Tiny now begins his agenda.)

SP: Was the marriage counselor able to help?

(In counseling we try to discourage too many direct questions since they tend to take the initiative away from the person who needs to talk. However, the student-pastor's question *does* indicate that Tiny has been heard.)

Tiny: Oh, I don't know. I talk to her more than I used to but I still won't fight with her. I guess that was part of the problem. I wouldn't fight with her and it made her mad.

(Tiny disposes of the direct question as quickly as possible and goes on to the second item on his agenda: the fact that he won't fight and that this makes his wife angry.)

SP: Do you suppose she just wanted your attention?

(The pastor cannot resist offering an interpretation of his wife's behavior. It is a likely interpretation, but it comes too quickly. Nevertheless, it is a response that indicates, once again, that the pastor *is* listening.)

Tiny: I don't know. You know I drive a truck and I leave at five in the evening and get home about four in the morning. So I sleep until late in the afternoon. Then I get up and eat and get ready to go to work. So I guess I don't have much time to talk to her.

(Tiny's disinterest in the pastor's premature interpretation is reflected in the casual way he disposes of the question and then hurries on to more of his agenda—the way he lives his life.)

SP: That is a pretty rough schedule. Do you have any children?

(In counseling, expressions of sympathy are usually to be discouraged. Perhaps Tiny has chosen this way of life for himself. If so, then why sympathize? The question regarding children is another direct one, but perhaps the pastor needs to know this to get a proper picture in his mind of the total situation.)

Tiny: Yes, a boy three years old and the baby is just fourteen months. And that's another thing—I made her quit work because she wasn't keeping the house up and taking care of the kids right. She was working at Penney's but the house and the kids come first.

(Again Tiny disposes of the direct question quickly and hastens on with more of his story. This shows his need for someone to listen to him.)

SP: I guess you don't have much time for the kids with your work schedule.

(For the first time the pastor resists the temptation to come up with a direct question. His response shows he has heard what Tiny has said.)

Tiny: Oh, I play with my little boy a little and we watch the cartoons on TV in the afternoons. But the baby is too small. I'm going home tomorrow morning and I'll be glad to see him. I've been in here five weeks now. My wife was in this afternoon and I told her to come early tomorrow morning and pick me up. I'll be glad to get home.

(Perhaps because the pastor's previous reply indicated interest and that he had been listening, Tiny now goes on to tell much more of his story, and the pastor learns many more things about him—his relationship with his child, his way of life, how long he has been in the hospital, and the fact that his wife is to come early the next morning and take him home.)

SP: I'm sure you will. That three-year-old son of yours will have grown some since you last saw him.

(Another response indicating Tiny has been heard.)

Tiny: Yeah, he's quite a kid. My wife is doing better about taking care of the kids but still not good enough. She stays up too late and then sleeps late in the morning. But the kids wake up early and sort of have to take care of themselves. I think she ought to go to bed early and get up with the kids and take care of them right.

(At this point the pastor must surely have been tempted to come in with a judgment. We are beginning to be sympathetic with a wife who has to live with such a judgmental and critical man. But the pastor bravely resists this temptation, although in his next response he cannot resist another direct question.)

SP: Is this the main problem between you and your wife that causes her to want to fight?

Tiny: I don't know. But you know when I get mad I could put my fist right through a wall or a door. I don't dare hit anybody. I just about killed two people once and ever since then I have to be careful.

(This shows the importance of listening. The pastor's direct question was premature again. Tiny did not yet have all of his agenda out. He needs to talk with someone about the awful memories he has of the unfortunate results of his bad temper. One could not have predicted that he had such a need. Only the listening process allows it to be revealed.)

SP: How did that happen?

(Perhaps the pastor said this with awe; to think of this huge man almost killing someone is awesome.)

Tiny: Well, when I was younger I was playing with these kids and I pushed one of them into a bush. The bush had some branches that had been broken off and the stubs were pretty sharp. And I guess I pushed this kid so hard that the stubs punctured his chest and throat. The other time a kid was teasing my brother, who is mentally retarded, and I picked him up and almost threw him off the bridge, but my mother stopped me just in time—but I was really going to throw him off the bridge. Anyway, that's why I don't fight with her or anyone anymore.

(So Tiny finally gets out this frightening story. It was a relief to have someone listen to him tell this tale. We wonder if anyone else has ever heard it? We also wonder if *his wife,* who is so frustrated because he will not fight, knows about this. Only by listening could this story emerge.)

SP: What do you do when you get mad?

(Another direct question. A better response might have been, "You have such bad memories of your anger that you are afraid to fight anymore." That would have allowed Tiny to proceed in any way he wished. Nevertheless, the pastor's question is intelligent enough to indicate to Tiny once again that he has been heard. Why does the pastor press Tiny with so many direct questions? Perhaps because he is anxious for a resolution of the problem. That is a constant danger in the listening process: to try to press for a solution or answer. But the only real answer to human problems lies in each person's capacity to sort things out for himself.)

Tiny: Oh, I just walk away and try to forget it. I did get mad the other day and had the telephone yanked out. I found out that my wife's girl friends were using my phone for long distance phone calls because my last bill had about $40.00 extra on it because of long distance calls. So I had it yanked out and that made my wife pretty mad, but I don't care.

(Each time Tiny reveals something of himself we are tempted to think, "Now that, surely, is the end of the story." But it isn't, and Tiny has not yet completed his agenda, so he goes on to tell of the phone call incident.)

SP: I can understand how you feel, but on the other hand a telephone is pretty important to have—especially in cases of emergencies, for example.

(For the first time the pastor interjects a parental note of advice or judgment. It was hard to resist since something in the pastor no doubt objected to Tiny's way of handling his difficulties with his wife and the phone. Nevertheless, it only makes Tiny defensive, as we see from his next response.)

Tiny: Yeah, I know, but I work hard for my money and I've been in this hospital and lost a lot of time. No, I won't hurt her, but I just may pack up and leave and go someplace where they will never find me.

(This is the little boy in Tiny speaking, the child who would run away from home because it has become too painful. Is it possible that the pastor's previous response, which was partly a parental rebuke, produced this regressive reaction

in Tiny? The pastor seems to have lost ground by his judgmental response. Once again he would have done better to
have simply listened. Tiny knows the value of telephones;
he did not need to be told that. But he cannot act differently because of his great built-up rage and anger. When he
gets all of this out, then Tiny can find more appropriate
ways of dealing with his problems.)

SP: Do you want to run away from your boys?

(Another direct question, but a shrewd one because it
brings Tiny out of his childish, regressive attitude, and
back to his mature, adult self. In Tiny's next, and last response, we can see the two sides of him—the childish, egocentric side and the mature side—wrestling with each
other.)

Tiny: No, I guess not, and I haven't done it yet. Maybe I
won't. I don't know.

The student-pastor explained that this ended the conversation because the doctor came in. He offered the following comments and interpretation of what happened, and also told us the
interesting sequel to his talk with Tiny:

> I really didn't have any solution for Tiny and I could
> feel his frustration and anger that he was afraid to show.
> Actually, I feel that the situation is rather explosive, es-
> pecially since Tiny and his wife are not able to sit down
> and talk things over. As in the great majority of cases,
> there is room for improvement on both sides.
>
> I could feel that Tiny wanted to get out of the hospi-
> tal, but on the other hand he was afraid the situation at
> home would be just as bad as it had been. I felt that he was
> feeling trapped and really didn't know what to do. I do
> believe that he knows he can't run away from the problem,
> even though that does have a strong appeal to him at times.

At least they did go to a marriage counselor once, and perhaps if the situation warrants it, they will try again. It would seem to me that several sessions would be required and they both would have to be legitimately willing to try much harder.

I was discharged from the hospital at 1:30 P.M. the next afternoon and my two sons came after me. As we left at 2:00 P.M. Tiny was still waiting for his wife to come and get him. He had been dressed since 9:00 A.M. as his wife had promised to come early. And, of course, he couldn't telephone her.

In spite of some mistakes, the student-pastor did a good job helping Tiny because he was, basically, a good listener. Tiny greatly needed this talk. His urge toward health was shown in his desire to talk to his hospital roommate as soon as he found out he was a minister. Tiny needs to talk much more to someone.

So far we have looked at this conversation from a professional angle, and I have analyzed the student-pastor's responses as a professional counselor. But the listening process, as stressed before, is not just what professionals do, but what people do for each other. The poignant ending to the story shows this, for at the end Tiny's wife does not show up. We cannot help but wonder if she is expressing her anger toward Tiny for tearing out the telephone. Clearly, Tiny and his wife need to talk with and listen to each other. When Tiny tore out the phone, and, presumably, when his wife failed to come to take him home, both were expressing themselves to the other indirectly. In a later chapter we will examine such indirect means of communication more closely. For the most part, such indirect ways of getting someone else to hear us run the risk of being destructive, and are last resorts taken because the usual attempts at communication have failed. When people do not listen to us, we find other ways to get the message across.

Chapter Four
Our Gigantic Emotions

Marie-Louise von Franz, a Jungian analyst from Zurich, in her book *The Shadow and Evil in Fairy Tales*, points out a number of interesting things about giants. She notes that giants appear in myths and fairy tales all over the world. They are very old, and are usually regarded in mythology as having been created by the gods before humankind, as though the gods first fashioned some clumsy, less successful type of humanoid being and then, having benefited from their experience, created human beings. In fact, in some mythology, such as the Norse, the giants antedated the appearance of the gods. It is also worth noting that in Norse mythology some giants were fire giants and some were ice giants—a point we will return to.

In Greek mythology, the role of the giants is taken over by the Titans, who existed before human beings and were the rivals of the Olympian gods. The Titans had gigantic strength. One of them was bound by the gods under Mount Etna, and whenever he rolled over it created a volcanic eruption. But at least one of the Titans—Prometheus—was creative and beneficial to mankind, for it was Prometheus who, at great risk to himself, stole fire from the gods and gave it to mankind.

In most fairy tales giants are destructive and dangerous. Fortunately they are also stupid, and so fairy tale heroes usually manage to outwit them. In this way a dangerous giant sometimes is transformed into a creative and helpful giant. This is the way it happened, for instance, in the story "The Spirit in the Bottle."

In this tale a young man is wandering through the woods and stops to rest at the base of a great tree. Here he finds a corked bottle from which a voice cries out, clamoring for release. The young man obligingly uncorks the bottle and immediately a tremendous genie rushes from his prison and threatens to devour him. But the clever young man saves himself by expressing disbelief that such a gigantic genie could ever have gotten himself into a tiny bottle. The genie, his pride injured, proves that he can perform such a feat by going back into the bottle again, and the young man quickly pops the cork back into place. Once more the genie clamors for release, but the young man refuses to let him out unless he agrees that he will not devour him, but will be his servant instead. The genie agrees, is released, and keeps his word. Because of his powerful servant, the young man is now able to become very successful in the world.

As von Franz points out, our uncontrolled emotions and affects are like giants, for they also threaten to devour us, and therefore are dangerous and destructive. We can say that giants personify overwhelming emotions that can get out of control and overpower the ego. Our ordinary language suggests this. We speak of a "gigantic emotion," or of someone being in a "towering rage." We might say of an angry person that "he erupted like a volcano," or that someone is "swallowed up in anger," or that a person's rage "boils over." We even personify our gigantic storms with personal names, calling our hurricanes Edna or Louise, and, in more recent, less chauvinistic times, Howard or Norman.

Like giants, such uncontrolled emotions also have a some-what stupid quality. Under their influence we lose perspective and cannot be reached by feeling or reason. For example, a frustrated child gets into a gigantic rage and has a temper tantrum that completely possesses him. Or someone makes a little remark to us that touches us in a sensitive spot and becomes a greatly exaggerated issue. A disappointed child, under the impetus of gigantic childish emotion, turns an ordinary disappointment of life into an enormous tragedy. And adults, under the impetus of inner giants, make mountains out of molehills, elephants out of lice, and turn minor difficulties into gigantic ones.

Then we have the Nordic fire and ice giants mentioned earlier. They are personifications of hot anger and cold anger. For instance, we say that someone does things in a "fiery rage," but we also speak of someone who has become "icy cold." The ice giants are the worst. If a person kills someone in hot anger, perhaps because of a personal quarrel or an unfortunate love affair, we are dismayed but we can understand it, and, in a corner of our heart, can even be sympathetic. But if someone has become cold-blooded and without emotion kills other people who are strangers to him, we feel we are in the presence of something truly evil and our human sensibilities are justifiably shocked. This is the ice giant, an anger that has been so deeply repressed that a person may not even know he is angry; he only knows that he is driven by a cold urge to kill.

Gigantic emotions are an impediment to communication for many reasons. Like giants, who are dangerous and destructive, we too, under the influence of a gigantic emotion, are apt to be dangerously unconscious. To return to our analogy of a game of catch, when controlled by a powerful affect our first throw is likely to be a ball thrown as hard as we can at the other person's head. We do not want him to catch the ball and return it; we want to hurt him. And should the other person succeed in catch-

ing the ball and returning it to us with a fair throw, we are likely
to continue to hurl the ball back as hard as we can. We miss the
point of what the other person has indicated by his throw because our gigantic anger has blinded us. It keeps us rigid, so we
are not able to enter into creative dialogue.

Moreover, emotions are contagious. If we begin communication under the impetus of a powerful emotion, a similar
emotion will be aroused in the other person. Rage creates rage,
affect brings out affect, one giant creates another. The resulting
exchange quickly becomes banal, generating more heat than
light, and being more destructive than constructive.

Perhaps worst of all, when we are in the grip of a gigantic
emotion we do not hear the other person. Our inflamed emotionality is like a huge wall, and the best thrown balls of the
other person bounce off of it. Only after the emotion has been
dissipated are we capable of hearing what another person is saying.

And yet, as mythology and fairy tales remind us, under
some circumstances giants can be enormously creative. Creative
work itself can be described as a "gigantic effort," and under the
impetus of great emotion people often perform heroic feats and
accomplish creative tasks. But in these cases the giant has been
put to work in the service of the personality and is not devouring
it. Like the spirit in the bottle, the ego is no longer overwhelmed;
a new center of gravity in the personality has changed things
around so that the gigantic emotions now work harmoniously for
the whole.

So we can't say all gigantic emotions should be repressed or
eliminated. Sometimes these towering emotions are needed in
order to have communication. They must be expressed, heard,
and understood. If they are denied, denigrated, or repressed, a
person not only loses the negative emotion but all emotions, not
just angry feelings but all feelings, not only destructive energy
but positive energy as well. So the ticklish task in interpersonal

communication is to allow the emotions without being over-whelmed and devoured by them. In fairy tale language, we must deal with the giants and overcome their negativity by becoming conscious. The ego, in short, must exercise its intelligence and not give in to blind emotions; yet at the same time we must work with the giants and honor them, for in the final analysis we can do nothing without them.

Having said we must work with and honor our emotional giants, let us examine what we can do to keep them from block-ing communication. There are no easy answers and no panaceas, but a few steps can be taken that may prove helpful.

The first step in such an emotional situation is to recognize the emotion and "keep our cool." If someone comes to us who is very angry or upset and we are in a position of strength and assurance, we can respond to the person's need positively and creatively.

One such response would be to help the other person by identifying and recognizing the emotion the other person is ex-pressing. Let us imagine a situation in which we are unavoidably detained and so arrive late for a luncheon engagement with a friend. Before we have a chance to explain, she greets us with a barrage of emotion, which we feel is somewhat unjustified be-cause we did not have a chance to offer our explanation. Recog-nizing the situation, we can say, "You are angry, and I am not surprised." This allows the other person to be angry at us. We do not put her down for being angry, but indicate that we under-stand it. Our friend may then continue, "Yes, I am angry ..." and proceed to tell us how she felt while waiting there feeling impatient and neglected. This defuses her anger and makes it possible for her to hear our explanation or apology, as the case may be. For after anger has been heard and recognized the chances for a productive discussion are greater.

This is a difficult thing to do. It is not easy to be confronted by an angry person and be able and willing to accept that anger without retaliating in kind. To listen to someone's anger, respond creatively, and expect nothing back in return is like giving her a gift, as noted earlier. It takes a lot of maturity to be able to do this, and is akin to what the New Testament calls "agape." We cannot expect to be able to do this all the time—or even very often—but when we can, it not only helps the other person, it helps us too. For by making a mature response in a difficult situation we become more mature. It is one of those situations in which you are what you do.

This is not to say that such a response is always the correct response. Every situation, every dialogue, every encounter between two people is unique. There may be situations in which the correct response is to get angry ourselves in response to the anger of someone else. Sometimes that is just what someone else needs to hear from us: our anger. What it does say is that it helps if we are capable of more than one response to emotion.

However, if we are the person who is upset about something, we cannot necessarily depend on the other person to be able to receive our anger in a positive and creative way. The chances are that the other person will not be sufficiently psychologically aware to deal with our anger creatively. Or the other person may not be feeling strong enough that day to accept the blast of our emotions without succumbing to his own. Sometimes, then, we can help the situation by doing something with our emotions first on our own, and then going to the other person. This way the gigantic emotion is not so likely to swallow us and prove a barrier to communication.

Such an acceptance of anger is just as important when relating to children as it is in relating to adults. If our child is angry it helps to acknowledge that with a simple, "You are very angry now." Children, like adults, need to have their feelings understood.

It also helps us as parents to be able to say to our children, "You are making me very angry." Children can accept the fact that their parents are angry at them if they know that the parents are acknowledging it. What is damaging to the child is the parent's unacknowledged, hidden anger.

In most instances, keeping the gigantic emotion from being a barrier to communication to adults or children is helped by writing in our journal about our emotion and our feelings. A journal is a notebook in which we keep a running record of the important things that go through our screen of consciousness each day. All kinds of things go into our journals: creative ideas that popped into our minds, our dreams, our reflections, and a record of our emotional responses to life situations. Ira Progoff has done a great deal to make us aware of the value of keeping a journal, and Morton T. Kelsey has written about keeping a journal in his fine book *Adventure Inward.* I have a section on it also in my book *Healing and Wholeness.*

Writing in our journal about people or situations that have evoked in us anger, anxiety, or a sense of defeat helps to stabilize our psychological situation and strengthen our ego. It helps us to "get a handle" on our emotions without repressing them, and to get a look at the giant that threatens to swallow us. If we do this before we get into a discussion that might become highly emotional, the chances are good that we can express our feelings to the other person and not be consumed by them. By writing things out in our journal, the gigantic emotion is diminished a bit, and the ego becomes proportionately larger and stronger. This enables us to make the opening toss of the ball more carefully and accurately and in a way that is less threatening to the other person.

A second way of dealing with our emotions before our discussion takes place is to talk the emotion over with another, objective person first. This other person might be a counselor, priest, minister, or a friend. The only qualification is that the other person be a good listener, be objective, and have enough self-knowledge that he does not leap in to give us bad advice or try to influence us to certain actions that are really dictated by his own situation or problems. (Let us say, for instance, that we are angry at our wife and talk it over with a friend who has just divorced. Because of his own circumstances, that person might urge us to divorce.) Discussing our emotions first with another person can have the same salutary effect as writing about them in our journal, except, of course, that we have the added benefit of the personal presence and support of our friend or counselor.

When emotion is likely to run high on both sides there is another way to initiate discussion that is sometimes helpful; this is by writing a letter or note. We usually think of writing a person a letter only when he is at a distance from us and we must use the mail instead of talking to him personally. But there are occasions when we may wish to write a note to someone who actually lives in the same house with us. If we write a person a letter about our present concern, it gives us the opportunity to express ourselves more clearly and objectively than might be possible if we spoke to him directly. If we are afraid that our gigantic emotions would rise up and overwhelm us in a negative way if we started to talk about the difficult matter, we might choose to start the dialogue with a note instead.

We might also choose to write a note when we think the other person might become highly emotional or upset at the issue we are going to raise. In this case, beginning with a note gives us a chance to phrase what we want to say carefully, and it gives the other person an opportunity to react privately to the message, digest its contents, and perhaps come up with a creative response on his own. When we write the note we must be available for a personal response and discussion afterward.

There are no rules about when it is preferable to initiate discussion in this way; however it is helpful to know there is more than one way to start a dialogue.

There is one caution about writing such a note: we must be careful that it is phrased in such a way that we do not care who sees it. It is always possible that the other person may choose to use our note as a weapon against us. This is especially the case if he is not trustworthy. I remember when I made a call in one of my parishes. The woman on whom I was calling produced a letter to her from the previous rector of the church in which he raised some issues with her and used some injudicious language. I was startled when I looked at the date on the letter to see that it had been written many years before. I could not help but wonder how many people had been shown this note.

Of course these suggestions will not work if the two people involved do not both have a certain measure of psychological honesty, a sense of fair play, and a desire to work things out. If people do not want to communicate, or fear the consequences of communication too deeply, they will find ways to avoid it no matter how resourceful we are in approaching them. We will want to give a person every opportunity to talk with us, but if we have played all fifty-two cards in our deck, as one woman once expressed it to me, with no results, then we may have to face the fact that this particular person is not going to communicate with us.

Chapter Five

The Anima/Animus Fight

There is a special instance of emotion that destroys communication which is so important that I must mention it in some detail, even though I have already described it in my book *The Invisible Partners*. This is the fight that can take place between the animus and the anima. The animus designates the masculine qualities in a woman, and the anima designates the feminine qualities of a man. Thus the kind of difficulty in communicating that I am discussing is one that develops between men and women, and that involves their inner, unconscious counterparts.

A woman's masculine qualities can be a very positive part of her personality, and so can a man's feminine qualities. The one acts like "spirit" and the other like "soul," enlivening life and opening up new horizons. I have presented and discussed these qualities in the book mentioned above, but the negative ones are what concern us here.

The animus, in his negative manifestation, is blunt, has inflexible opinions, caustic and moralistic judgments, is brutal, and has a certain amount of unpleasant aggressiveness. If a woman is taken over negatively by this side of her nature we refer to her as "animus-possessed," and she will display the above-mentioned qualities in her relationships with other people. It is as though her masculine side, which properly belongs inside of her, from which point it lends strength to her character, has gotten outside of her, in between her and other people. This is the wrong place for the animus and mischief is the result.

Likewise the anima, in her negative manifestations, displays undesirable qualities. She shows herself in moodiness, sulkiness, pettiness, and in her capacity to poison the man and everyone else around her by creating a bad effect. Negatively, she acts for all the world like an inferior, peevish, overly sensitive woman. If she takes a man over we refer to him as "animapossessed." Such a man falls into dark moods that make him unapproachable by others. He loses his objectivity, and all difficulties in emotionally toned relationships become greatly enlarged. Small hurts, when magnified by the anima, become huge personalistic issues which she feels compelled to avenge. The weapons of the anima are mood, emotionality, and poisonous comments which she inflicts upon those who have aroused her ire. If only the man can get this feminine side of himself in the proper place, which is inside, and give her the right attention, all goes well. But if the anima gets between a man and other people, there is the devil to pay! For she then exaggerates all difficulties, falsifies situations, intensifies hurts, and turns relationships with members of the other sex either into dramatic love affairs that soon crash to the ground, or dramatic witch-hunts.

To make matters worse, the anima in a man has a way of evoking the animus in a woman, and vice versa. In other words, the two do not like each other, and one brings out the worst in the other.

As C. G. Jung once said, no man can talk with a woman's animus for more than five minutes without falling victim to his own anima. The opinionated comments of the animus, and the brutal, unfeeling words he puts into a woman's mouth, soon infuriate the man's anima. He becomes as possessed as she is and a battle royal develops. In this dramatic but pointless battle the anima resorts to her weapons of poison and emotionality, and the animus draws his sword of power and criticism. But if a man cannot listen to the animus without falling a victim to his anima, neither can a woman stand a man's anima. For as soon as a man is swallowed up in his anima he is no longer in relationship, and this is unbearable.

The battle of the anima and animus may be dramatic and it may be royal, but it is not enlightening. The encounter is characterized by intense emotion, which turns into affect as each person becomes possessed by a dark and archetypal rage. In fact, the man and woman are hardly there at all now; instead their inner counterparts, the anima and animus, are having a furious encounter. This represents a defeat for the ego of both the man and the woman, and with the resulting lowered threshold of consciousness and discrimination both of them may say terrible things they later regret, or even may do physical damage to each other.

In short, the anima/animus battle is destructive, and no communication comes out of it. What might have been a playful and helpful game of catch now becomes a shouting match, and the original pair, the man and woman, are now in the background while a second pair, dark and full of blind affects, has taken over the stage.

The sad thing is that the whole dark encounter might have been avoided if the man or woman had expressed the proper feeling in the first place. The inner partners, the anima and animus, usually take over when there is a hurt feeling that has not been expressed openly and directly in the relationship. For instance, a man gets his feelings hurt, but for one reason or another says nothing about it. The hurt feeling does not go away. It simply drops into the unconscious, and there in the basement of his mind is the anima, who seizes upon that hurt, enflames it, enlarges it, and plots revenge. Had the man had the courage or forethought to bring up the disturbing matter directly in the first place, the anima would never have gotten hold of it. Then communication could have taken place and something could have been worked out.

It is the same with a woman. Her animus takes her over when she has a hurt feeling she has not let herself express. She tries to bury it, disregard it, or make it go away, but her inner man only gets hold of it and makes a cause out of it. He will have revenge!

Sometimes when the anima/animus battle starts it is because a succession of hurts have been repressed. A man makes a habit of not dealing with his feelings, and if he is slighted or wounded he just drops the little demon through a trap door into the lower level. But one day he drops another hurt into the basement and this time, before he can close the trap door, all the repressed, hurt feelings he has placed in there come bursting out. Made witchlike by the man's repression of her, the anima has nourished each hurt feeling carefully and they have now become full-fledged devils just aching to wreak destruction and achieve revenge. The anima now possesses the man and lets her devils loose.

The rule is, then, that if we want to communicate we must work with our own feelings. We cannot just shove them into the unconscious. We must learn to bring them out openly with each other. If this is not possible, we must work with them consciously by writing them in our journal, or we should talk them over with a friend or counselor. And we might do all three.

The Second Book of Samuel[1] has a story of an anima/animus fight that is instructive. When the Philistines conquered the Israelites they took away the holy Ark of the Lord. When David became king he defeated the Philistines and sent men to bring

---

[1] Quotations for this story are from The Jerusalem Bible.

the Ark back to the Citadel of David. As the bearers of the Ark of Yahweh are entering the city, David goes out to meet them, naked except for a loin cloth, and as the Ark is paraded through the excited populace David performs an ecstatic, whirling dance while everyone shouts and the musicians sound their horns.

Meanwhile Michal, one of David's wives and a daughter of Saul, is watching all this from the palace window. We are told that when she sees the naked David leaping and dancing in the street she "despised him in her heart." In other words, she did not think this was proper behavior for a king.

Eventually the religious ceremonies are over and David comes back to the privacy of his home. There Michal greets him, saying sarcastically, "What a fine reputation the King of Israel has won himself today, displaying himself under the eyes of his servants' maids, as any buffoon might display himself" (2 Sam. 6:20).

In response to this thrust David retaliates, first with a defensive remark, and then with vindictiveness: "I was dancing for Yahweh, and not for them. As Yahweh lives, who chose me in preference to your father and his whole House to make me a leader of Israel, Yahweh's people, I shall dance before Yahweh and demean myself even more. In your eyes I may be base, but by the maids you speak of I shall be held in honor" (2 Sam. 6:21).

The story has this sad ending: "And to the day of her death, Michal, the daughter of Saul, had no children." In other words, David refused to sleep with her. I say this is sad because Michal deserved a better fate. After all, it was she who saved David's life from her father's jealous rage many years before at great risk to herself. But a man in an anima mood has a short memory when it comes to past blessings.

Let us conjecture how this unfortunate encounter came about, studying the story with the help of what we know of the anima and animus.

The difficulty begins when Michal disapproves of David's nakedness and public dancing. The animus is full of opinions about how things *should* be, and is always ready to advance these opinions without regard to the feelings of the other person. Let us say that a man is enamored of his bright, new red shirt and puts it on with his orange tie to go to a party. Then along comes his wife's animus who says to him disdainfully, "You aren't going to wear *that* combination, are you!" The man is punctured, wounded, and feels like a hurt little boy. But he says nothing, takes off the shirt and tie and puts on a white shirt and brown tie, and off they go to the party. Later his wife wonders why he is so cold to her during the evening and talks to everyone but her. She has forgotten her brief animus attack on him and is ready for a good time, and is hurt because he ignores her. It never occurs to her that his anima is punishing her animus for the wounding attack.

David has come home in a fine mood. He has defeated the Philistines and has now enjoyed an exciting triumph. It was thrilling to dance before the Ark and have all the maids of Israel admire his masculine body as he trooped through the city streets. Michal not only disapproved, but was wounded that he would want to make himself attractive to other women and not reserve all of that fine masculine display for her. But she starts with the animus rather than with her feelings. She might have said, "It was a glorious triumph, David, but I felt ignored and left out when you danced before all those other women." But she didn't, and the sword-thrust from her animus came out instead.

Had David been in a calmer frame of mind he might have kept his cool and gotten to the bottom of the matter. He could have said, "Michal, what is really bothering you?" or even, "It hurts my feelings when you say that." But he was already in an anima mood when he entered the palace, only it was an inflated mood that he was enjoying. Michal's animus pricked his balloon neatly and completely, and David did not like it. He immediately fell into his anima. Notice that in his reply to Michal he refers disparagingly to her father, Saul, and his whole household, and flaunts it in her face that Yahweh chose him over her own father's household. This is not fair since, as noted earlier, it was Michal herself who chose David rather than Saul many years ago when she assisted David in escaping from her father's soldiers. But the anima, when she seeks revenge for an injury, is not interested in being fair, and thinks nothing of personalistic attacks that have nothing to do with the issue.

When David goes on to say, "I *shall* dance before Yahweh and demean myself even more," he sounds like a little boy defying his mother. He is so afraid of being dominated by his wife, who has suddenly in his eyes become his mother, that he reacts as far as he can in the other direction. If she says not to dance he will dance twice as much!

In this case David, being the king, has more guns than Michal. He is able to reject her and leave her childless, and so vindictive is the anima, and so persevering is her poisonous affect, which can nurse a grudge for years, that David's punishment of her is permanent.

The story of David and Michal has a sad ending, and many encounters between men and women today have a sad ending too, and unnecessarily so. For when the anima and animus take over in the way I have described, communication ceases and a difficulty that could have been worked through creatively, had the man and woman communicated with each other without interference from their inner partners, has now become a gigantic obstacle. The sad part is that it doesn't have to happen this way.

Chapter Six

The Proteus Problem

Among the fabulous beings of Greek mythology was Proteus, the "Old Man of the Sea," whose duty was to guard the herd of seals that belonged to Poseidon. Each day at noon Proteus would emerge from the watery depths to rest upon the rocks, while the herd of seals gathered around him. Now was the time when an enterprising person could learn from him, for Proteus had the gift of looking into the future and spoke only the truth. There was a problem, however: Proteus was a shape-shifter. He could assume any shape he desired: lion, dragon, water, fire, tree ... And when asked a question, instead of answering, Proteus would change shape. This was enough to frighten and discourage most people, but if you persisted, and especially if you hung on to Proteus resolutely no matter what shape he assumed, eventually he would be forced to assume his human form and give you the answer to your question.

People can be shape-shifters too. When we approach them for a straight answer, instead of giving us one, like Proteus they twist and turn into different shapes as fast as you can blink an eye. When people say something but you are not quite sure what they are saying, when they are confronted by a certain issue but manage to change the conversation to a different issue, when they leave us confused amidst a cloud of innuendo—then they are playing Proteus. It is enough to confuse and intimidate the bravest among us—unless we realize what is going on, screw our courage to the sticking-place (as Shakespeare would say), and hang on.

People tend to turn Proteus on us under two conditions: first, when we are trying to communicate with them about a matter that is disconcerting or painful to them; second, when they want to tell us something and do not want to take responsibility for it.

It took some doing to make Proteus stop shifting shapes and assume his proper form, and it takes some doing to make people stop playing Proteus games with us. There are three common ways Proteus games are played. Examining these will help us see how frustrating it is to us when we want to communicate and the other person plays Proteus; it will also give us some ideas on what we can do about it.

The first example is called "Shifting the Ground." Let us say that Mary wants to bring up a certain matter with John. We will call this matter "A." However, John finds this a painful matter to discuss, for it points a finger at some error he has made, some fault or failure of relationship with Mary. Or maybe John simply does not like any kind of emotionally charged discussion. So when Mary brings up matter "A" John quickly brings up matter "B." Instead of dealing with what Mary wants to discuss he diverts the discussion to another subject.

"John," Mary begins, "I need to talk with you about something. I thought we already decided on the blue wallpaper for the bedroom, that kind I especially liked. But then you went ahead and without even telling me you bought the yellow wallpaper. This makes me feel that my ideas about things don't count with you."

John, feeling uncomfortable about this, answers, "Well what

about last week, when I asked you to go by the library for me and get those books, and you forgot all about it? How do you think that made me feel?"

Mary suddenly feels upset. First, she is vaguely frustrated and resentful because the matter she brought up is not being discussed. Second, she feels attacked by John, who has brought up the matter of the library. The chances are that she will be more aware of the second feeling than the first. She will take John's defensive counter to her opening comment as his assuming the offensive, and accordingly she will feel threatened and attacked.

She may now do two things. First, especially if her self-image is not too great, she might defend herself about the matter of the library. Of course that will please John. He can then go on to discuss *that* subject rather than the matter of the wallpaper, and Mary can be the one feeling uncomfortable. By the time they get through hashing over the library incident there will be no time or energy left for the matter Mary wanted to discuss. John can trot off happily to work in the garden. His security and egocentricity were momentarily threatened by Mary, but his clever Proteus found a way out of it. However, Mary will be left frustrated, unrelated to her husband, and perhaps down on herself. As John closes the door behind him, she probably hears a negative thought inside her saying, "You see, these things are all your fault," or, "Oh well, it doesn't matter. It isn't that important."

If Mary's self-image is strong she may react a little differently to John when he brings up the other matter. Instead of defending herself she may angrily retort with another accusation. In response to "B" she now brings up "C," saying, "Well, I am not the only one to forget things. How about the time I left the car at the garage and you were to pick me up but got so busy at your work that you forgot. I was standing there waiting for an hour!"

John would have preferred that Mary defend herself against his accusation about the library. But he is not too upset, for he has a better answer for this matter than he had for the matter of the wallpaper. "I have told you a hundred times," he says with characteristic exaggeration, "that when I get to the office things begin to happen and I cannot always keep my schedule. I even told you that day when you went to the garage that if the boss called me I would have to talk to him first before I could pick you up."

As you can imagine, from here the conversation deteriorates rapidly. Any semblance of communication has ceased. The playful game of catch has become a shooting contest. And Mary is the loser because the matter she wanted to discuss has not been talked about. John has won this confrontation and may even leave for the garden feeling good about himself. We are apt to feel smug when someone touches our Shadow (the weak or dark side of our personality) and we are clever and manage to escape.

What might Mary have done? Perhaps she could have remembered Proteus and not let John escape. To do this she would have had to (1) have clearly in mind what it was that she wanted to discuss; (2) refuse to go into any other subject until the matter she wanted to discuss was dealt with; (3) see what John was trying to do in order to escape.

When John brought up his counter remark about the library, she might have replied, "If you want to talk about that we can discuss it later. First I want to talk about the wallpaper." No doubt John will try again, and maybe again, to escape, but if Mary hangs on resolutely he may be forced at long last to deal with the issue. Of course he may refuse to. Perhaps he will stalk out of the house angrily. If Mary's self-image is low she may hear her negative voice say, "You see, you just didn't approach him in the right way." Not at all! She must put this voice aside as resolutely as she put aside John's Proteus maneuvers. She approached the matter correctly. John is angry because his egocentric maneuvers to escape a painful discussion did not work. He is upset because he did not win. As for Mary, she will still be upset with John, as she should be for his evasive behavior, but not with herself. For she knew what her ground was and succeeded in holding to it.

In this hypothetical illustration of how the game of "Shifting the Ground" is played, it was Mary who brought up the difficult matter and John who played Proteus. But women can play Proteus too. I once counseled a lawyer who had great difficulty discussing things with his wife because she would shift shapes and change the subject cleverly whenever he tried to bring up some difficult matter. One day I said to him, "Tom (not his real name), you are a lawyer. Suppose you have a witness on the stand and you say to him, 'And where were you on the night of the 4th of July?' And suppose your witness answered, 'Well, I don't want to talk about the 4th of July, but on November 1st I was in Las Vegas.' What would you say?" And Tom answered, "Of course I would say, 'Answer the question!'" "Okay," I replied, "if you would not let a witness get away with this, why do you let your wife get away with it?"

When Tom returned the next week he told me that when he next approached his wife for a talk he brought a pad and pencil with him. After he broached his opening problem with her, and she started to reply, he began to write things down busily. At last she interrupted her flow of talk and said, "What are you doing?" Tom replied, "Writing down all the things we have to talk about *after* we have talked about the matter I first brought up." Fortunately Tom's wife had a good sense of humor. She saw the ridiculousness of the situation and laughed. They both had a good laugh, in fact, and the discussion went on to a positive and amicable conclusion. Not all such exchanges turn out this well, but they don't all turn out badly either.

A second Proteus game is called "The Bird in the Bushes." Let us say you are walking through the woods when you hear a rustling in the bushes. It sounds like a small animal or a bird. Then you hear some chirping, and a fluttering sound, like wings. "Well," you conclude to yourself, "if it chirps like a bird, and flutters like a bird, it probably *is* a bird." Probably you are right, but of course you could be mistaken. If you want to be absolutely sure, you will have to poke into the bushes and see for yourself.

Sometimes people say something to us that is like a bird in the bushes. They cleverly conceal what they actually mean, but we are left with a distinct impression that they are trying to tell us something unpleasant about ourselves, criticize us in some way, or depreciate us in a subtle manner. These people hide their true meaning carefully, but manage to phrase their comment with such an innuendo that it leaves a disagreeable effect upon us. It is a way people have of affecting other people without having to take responsibility for it. They hide in the bushes, so to speak, and let us have it as we pass by, and we are wondering what happened. The chances are that by the time we have worked through our impressions to some kind of awareness, they are long gone. We are left with an uncomfortable or hurt feeling, but they have gotten away scot-free.

However, we do not have to be the helpless victim of this kind of manipulation. We can take the innuendo we have felt and ask outright if that is what the other person meant. We might say, "Are you trying to tell me such-and-such?" This bold and direct approach will certainly take the other person by surprise. She has played this game many times and it has always worked before. Now suddenly she is being called to account for what she said. She is being asked to disavow something, or acknowledge it. Under these circumstances the person might say, "Yes, that is what I meant. I really did mean such-and-such." Now it is out in the open. It is disagreeable, but it can be dealt with; communication is possible.

Chances are, however, that this will not be the reply. It is not easy for us to own up to the shadowy remarks we have made.

If this is the case, the person playing Bird in the Bushes may make a denial: "Well of course that is not what I meant. I would never say such a thing!" Okay, we can leave it at that. We may suspect that is not really the case, but we do not have to press the issue. We can now reply, "I am certainly glad to hear that. For a moment I thought you were thinking such-and-such about me." Of course the issue is not resolved, but we feel better and the other person can feel a little uncomfortable now.

Let us take an example. Sarah, we will call her, goes to visit her mother, Mrs. Brown. Things are going well right now with Sarah. After an initial unhappy marriage that ended in divorce, the younger woman recently made a fortunate marriage. Her new husband is older than she is, but not too much older; he loves her, is financially successful, and is in every way a good catch. She is very happy with her new husband, and for the first time feels as though she loves a man. She likes this new feeling, and is even content to give up her work, which had become boring to her anyway, and, at least for the time being, devote herself to fixing up their home and making life comfortable for her husband. He likes it this way. He makes plenty of money and does not need her additional income. What he does need is her feminine presence and warmth. It is a good match and everyone is happy.

Everyone, that is, but Mrs. Brown. Her love life has ended badly—a divorce after many years of an unhappy marriage. Now she is well into middle-age and it is hard to find available and attractive men. Of course her daughter's husband would have been just about the right age for her, but he married the daughter, not her. Moreover, now that her marriage is over she has to work. Her work is really not too unpleasant, but the fact is that she *has* to do it. And there is her daughter who doesn't have to work and can do just as she pleases.

Of course the mother says none of this to her daughter directly. For one thing they live hundreds of miles apart. For another thing, the mother never brings things up directly. But now her daughter is here visiting her. The two of them naturally begin talking about what they are doing in their lives, and pretty soon the mother says, "Of course, your life is *different* than mine" (with emphasis on "different").

The daughter immediately has a funny sensation. It is a little as though a barb has suddenly hit her in the stomach. Suddenly, inexplicably, she feels guilty, and also depressed. In fact, though she has not yet thought of it, she feels quite a bit like the way she used to feel as a little girl when mother would say something to her that made her feel bad about herself. For reasons that are not clear to her, what started out as an ordinary conversation with her mother has turned dark, and her positive feeling of anticipation about the visit has turned into a depression. Since she doesn't know what to say next the daughter almost breaks off the talk completely. But then she remembers: This has happened to her before with her mother—many times.

Sarah allows herself a moment's reflection. What *did* her mother say to her? Was it a simple comment about the two lives being different? No, there was a subtle but unmistakable innuendo in the way her mother said it. The innuendo was: "You, of course, have life much easier than I do. I have a miserable lot in life, while you have everything you could want. And you should feel guilty about that."

There it is—the bird in the bushes! To be sure, her mother did not actually say that to her in so many words. But it *felt* as though that was her real meaning. "If it chirps like a bird, and flutters like a bird, it must be a bird." It felt for all the world as though her mother was trying indirectly to express her own disappointment she could not cope with, to put some of her bitterness off onto her daughter, and to make her own unhappiness a little more bearable by destroying Sarah's happiness.

Sarah decided that for her own well-being, and the well-being of the relationship, she would have to go into the bushes and see if a bird was really there. So instead of letting the matter drop she answered her mother, "When you say that my life is different than yours, are you trying to say that I have it easy while you have it hard, and that there is something wrong about that?"

Of course that is exactly what the mother meant to say, but she can't bring herself to own up to it. It would sound so dark and dreadful to admit that her seemingly simple remark had such a nasty, shadowy thrust to it. Maybe later she will admit it to herself, but now she cannot face it, and certainly cannot acknowledge it to her daughter. So she answers, "Oh no, I didn't mean anything like that. Of course I am happy that things are going so well for you."

Sarah is unconvinced. No doubt about it, that bird flew away, but just as it did she got a glimpse of it. Yes, her mother is quite capable of that kind of manipulation. Because she cannot face her own dark thoughts and disappointments she puts them on other people this way. But that is not the total picture of her mother. There is also her loving and concerned side. So Sarah decides not to push the matter any further, but neither will she be the unhappy, guilty little child. She is an adult now too, an equal to her mother. So she replies, "Well, I am glad to hear that. For just a moment I thought you were trying to tell me that there was something bad about the fact that my husband and I are so happy together."

The matter is dropped. The two go on to discuss safer subjects, and now the visit goes well. For one thing, the daughter feels on top, good about herself. And her mother has decided to be nicer too. They spend several days together without one more bird appearing in the bushes. It made the mother uncomfortable when it was flushed out like that. She isn't going to take any more chances, and resolves not to do that again. She has her nasty and inferior side, but she isn't a hateful person; she really loves her daughter and wishes her well.

On the whole, men are more likely than women to shift the ground, and women more likely than men to play the subtle game of the bird in the bushes. But both men and women play the third Proteus game, "You Shouldn't Feel Like That."

Earlier I suggested that a good way to begin communication was with an expression of feeling because this is less likely to arouse a defensive reaction in the other person, and more likely to begin the communication on the proper level. In terms of our image of the game of catch, it helps us begin the game with a playful, accurate, and not-too-hard toss of the ball.

But for those persons who like to play Proteus, there may be a quick shift of the ground from feeling to thinking, from communicating to arguing. And the sly way to do this is to turn the feeling itself into a matter of argument by attempting to discredit it.

Let us see how that works. John is upset because when he came home from work he found that his wife's sister was visiting, and his wife, instead of giving him her usual warm greeting, virtually ignored him. He knows it is pretty sensitive of him to let this offend him, but the fact is that it hurt his feelings and made him feel that he was unimportant in his wife's eyes. So he musters up his courage and finally says, "You know, Mary, I need to tell you that when I came home last night and you were so attentive to your sister it made me feel as though you didn't care about me, and that you were not happy to see me come home." And Mary answers, "Oh but you shouldn't feel like that."

Or let us say that Mary is upset with John because, when she tried to discipline their son, Jimmy, her husband jumped in and contradicted her. So she says, "You know, John, when you contradict me in front of the children when I am trying to discipline Jimmy, it makes me feel very unsupported." And John replies, "But you have no right to feel that way about it. This is an open family and we all say what we want to. You ought not to feel the way you do."

The chances are good that John, in the first example, and

Mary, in the second one, will quickly be pulled into an argument about whether or not their feeling has a right to be what it is. Proteus has worked again, for the ground of discussion has been shifted from feeling to thinking, from emotion to an argument. Moreover, if one person is better with words than the other, someone is going to lose, and the loser will think, "I guess I was just a stupid person to have felt that way." And yet the feeling, denigrated though it is, persists, and becomes the fuel for a growing resentment, or a growing self-depreciation, or both.

Such a shifting tactic is frequently employed by people who are uncomfortable in the area of feeling and emotion. In a later chapter we will see that those people we call "thinking types" are especially prone to shift the ground quickly, if they can, from feeling to an argument in order to use psychological faculties that enable them to feel superior. More often than not, it is the man who puts down the feeling of the woman and uses this particular Protean tactic, but not always, for women can play that game too. In our particular culture, in which thinking is overvalued and feeling is undervalued, it is especially easy to convince many people that their feelings have no validity, and to dismiss an attempt at communication with a "But you shouldn't feel that way."

Fortunately, it is possible for a person who expresses feeling to avoid being defeated in this matter by remembering one small thing: Feelings are facts, and as such they are not arguable, nor do they have to be justified, for they simply *are*. Feeling people do not need to let Proteus get away with it. All they have to do is to stick with their feelings.

In our first example, John might answer Mary by saying, "Well, maybe I shouldn't feel that way about it, but the fact is that I do." And in the second example, Mary might reply, "You may not think it is right, but the fact is that this is the way I feel." Or even, "How do you know how I should feel?"

Feelings are facts of relationship. It is our feelings that need to be discussed most of all. Feelings cannot be eliminated by shoulds, oughts, or arguments. Feelings do not have to be defended, but they do have to be faced, both by the person who has the feelings, and by the person with whom one is trying to communicate.

It takes a certain amount of strength to insist on the validity of one's feelings and not be drawn into arguments about their rightness or wrongness. But if a person sees what is happening when the other person disparages her feelings, and makes up her mind not to feel guilty about them, the strength usually comes.

However it is essential *to see what is happening.* In fact, in order to avoid being drawn into all the Proteus games we need to see them coming. Proteus succeeds because we do not see what is going on. Once we see what is happening, we have certain options at our disposal: We have a power of choice and we need not be the victim of someone else's ploy. This gives us a chance to save ourselves from being injured, and sometimes it saves the discussion as well.

But to see what is happening we need to keep a sentry posted. We need to detach a portion of our awareness and set it aside where it is in a position to see what is happening in a personal transaction. This sentry can then keep us informed of what Protean games may be developing. We need to be like prairie dogs, who always have a sentry on guard watching. While the other prairie dogs are busy doing whatever they are supposed to be doing this sentry is busy looking around; when danger comes he gives the signal, and all scurry for cover. Fortunately the ego can do this. The ego has a neat trick: It can be very involved in something, and still have a portion of itself standing outside the action, looking on objectively, and able to report to "central intelligence" what is going on.

It is unfortunate, but when communication is frustrated the

situation can become warlike. The idea of the sentry is to keep the warfare from spreading by reporting unfair tactics at the very beginning of communication. Then the war can be quickly halted and the creative game of communication can begin.

We've mentioned the matter of feeling guilty several times. Now we will look further into this matter of guilt.

Chapter Seven
Guilt and Communication

As we observed in the first chapter, most people have difficulty accepting guilt. Yet in the examples of the Proteus-like
games that we have just discussed, guilt played an important
role. People may play "Shifting the Ground" because they cannot stand to feel guilty. The matter that their partner brings up
may arouse a guilty feeling in them, so instead of talking it out
with their partner they shift the ground to something else. Simi-
larly we play "The Bird in the Bushes" when we want to make
the other person feel guilty or put down. The vague but powerful
innuendo that comes from the bushes is calculated to arouse an
uneasy feeling of guilt in the other person, to leave her with the
impression that something is wrong with her. This enables us to
substitute control and manipulation for communication. But if
the other person does not accept that guilt and responds directly
and openly, the game is up and perhaps real communication can
begin.

Guilt makes us uncomfortable, reduces us to unpleasant,
childlike feelings, and lowers our self-image so much that we do
not like it. As a result, whenever anything comes up in communication that awakens a sense of guilt we are apt to retreat, or
come back with a counter-accusation.

It is clear, then, that if we can learn to deal with guilt we can communicate more successfully. This means learning to accept guilt when it belongs to us, and to refuse it if it is not ours. So we have to begin by discussing the difference between *real* guilt and *false* guilt. The former we need to accept because it belongs to us. The latter we need to reject because it is not ours.

Let us start with false guilt. False guilt stems from our inner accusing voice. Everyone has such an inner accusing voice. When we hear it, it is like listening to an autonomous series of thoughts that go on in our minds and criticize or judge us, and generally put us down. It can be likened to an inner judge who observes all our actions and thoughts and, at the slightest opportunity, jumps in with a negative comment. Both men and women have such a guilt-producing voice. For reasons I go into in *The Invisible Partners*, the accusing voice in a man is apt to sound like a woman's voice and in a woman it is apt to sound like a man's voice.

It usually takes a little introspection to realize that such a voice is there. The reason for this is that the accusing voice has been there for so long we do not realize what it is doing to us. Chances are that we have heard such judgmental thoughts ever since we were a child. So it never occurs to us to think of these thoughts as coming from some part of ourselves that is different from our ego. This is all the more the case if we have become identical with those critical thoughts. Then they have swallowed us, so to speak. The result is a marked lowering of our self-image, a chronic feeling that we are not a good person, a depression, a lack of spontaneity, and a greatly reduced scope of living.

Often the guilt-producing thoughts can be traced back to their source in mother or father. Perhaps the thoughts started when mother or father let us know that sometimes we were a bad child who did bad things. There was the time when we walked through the irresistible puddles of water that were left from the beautiful rainstorm only to have father become angry at us because we had on our good shoes. There were the times

when we used the bad words the older children in the neighborhood used—we hardly knew what they meant—only to have
mother tell us that we had terrible thoughts and must never say
those things again. Or perhaps we had a father who went into
bad moods when we did things he did not like, and then would
not speak to us, or a mother who was an expert at conjuring up
an air of disapproval that convinced us that we were a malicious
boy or girl who was responsible for her unhappiness. In all these,
and a thousand other ways, a child can learn that she is not a
good person, and that love is always contingent on winning the
approval of critical parents.

The inner accusing voice may begin in such a way, but the
fact is that however much mother or father may have contributed to the problem it is ours now. Once we are grown it does no
good to blame mother or father for our problem; it now belongs
to us and we have to deal with it. Moreover, strange as it may
sound, we would have such an inner accusing voice anyway. To
be sure, if we had perfect parents we might have more self-con-
fidence, but everyone has such an inner voice regardless of the
kind of parents he had. This is because it is archetypal, which
means it is a typical, universal quality of the human mind to
have such a judgmental voice as part of one's personality struc-
ture. Nor does it benefit us as much as we might think to ana-
lyze the origin of the negative script back to our parents. True,
this gives us some historical perspective on our situation and that
is helpful, but it does not reduce the intensity of the inner accusations one iota. To win the battle against the accusing voice
requires a struggle in the here and now.

So how *can* we overcome the negative affects of the accusatory thoughts? As with most spiritual and psychological matters
there are no fixed rules and no set prescriptions everyone can
follow. Each person must find his own way. But there are a few
suggestions that are often helpful.

First, it helps to identify the accusing voice as clearly as
possible. To do this we need to pay attention to the thoughts that

enter our screen of consciousness so we become aware of the critical voice within us. This brings the critical voice out into the open and prevents it from poisoning us with guilty feelings about ourselves.

Second, we can pay close attention to the accusing thoughts so that we can identify exactly what the accusations against us are; no more vague but annihilating feelings of guilt! It helps at this point to write these thoughts in our journal, perhaps even putting quotation marks around them. The more clearly we identify the negative thoughts the more we separate ourselves from them.

Third, we can share the accusing thoughts with a trusted friend, priest or counselor. By sharing these thoughts with a fellow human being with whom we can speak frankly without fear of being judged, we will strengthen our ego and further diminish the power of the critic within us. This will also relieve our sense of isolation, and will help us feel like a more acceptable person.

Finally, we can learn to dialogue with the accusing voice, to talk back to it. This technique is called "active imagination," and I have described it more completely in the last chapter of my book *Healing and Wholeness*, and also in the appendix to my book *The Invisible Partners*. Look at it this way: You are already hearing a lot of "talk" going on in your mind, directed against you by your Inner Critic. Now learn to stop, note what is being said, and talk back to those thoughts. It is a good idea even to write down the ensuing "imaginary" conversation. This will make it all the more real to us. I put "imaginary" in quotation marks because it may seem like our imagination when we do this, but talking to such an inner voice is just as real as talking to an outer person. If you decide to do this, disregard the thought that says to you, "Oh you are only making this up." This thought also comes from the Inner Critic. It is his attempt to remain concealed and not be forced to give up his power.

This brings up the question of the relationship between the accusing voice and what we can call the voice of our real Self, the contrast between the Inner Critic and our true Conscience. After all, are we not supposed to have a Conscience? Is there not supposed to be something like God's voice within us that admonishes us when we do evil and tries to keep us on the right path in life? Of course. The problem is that the accusing voice poses as the true moral authority but isn't. That is one thing that gives the accusing voice such power: it acts as if it were God, and pretends to be our true Conscience. But it isn't, and there is one way we can tell: The accusing voice of which I am speaking can only be destructive. It has no power to build us up, or lead us to our true Self. It can only tear us down, and will infallibly say things that are annihilating. Its admonitions are full of "shoulds" and "oughts" and are phrased in generalities that condemn us as a person. They are the sort of accusations that leave us with the feeling "I guess I am just no good . . . I guess I am just a failure." In short, though this voice seems to be like God's it acts more like the devil of the New Testament whose name in Greek, *diabolos,* means "the accuser."

There is indeed a true Conscience within us, a voice that can be said to come from our real Self and that tries to correct us when we deviate from our proper path in life. When this voice comes to us we need to listen. But corrections from this voice do not annihilate us. Painful though such corrections may be, they lead us back to our true Self, not away from it. For these corrections come, not from false guilt feelings, but from a violation of our true and deepest nature. When we deviate from our true nature, we hear what amounts to the voice of God within us. This is our true Conscience, which may even speak to us in our dreams, as I have indicated in my book *Dreams and Healing.* The guilt we then become aware of is real guilt. We really are guilty when we go against our own nature. We need to accept this guilt as our own, for it belongs to us. We may not like it, but it is ours. But there is this redeeming fact: While false guilt diminishes our personality, real guilt does not. When we assume false guilt we are destroyed by it, but when we honestly carry the guilt that belongs to us we become bigger, not smaller, in personality.

Of course it is painful. Any guilt is painful. We do not want to acknowledge our real guilt. We even prefer our false guilts to our real guilts because, for reasons that we will investigate, the former allow us to retain our egocentricity, but the latter require us to give it up. We complain about both kinds of guilt, but we are secretly in alliance with the false guilt. Yet it is the real guilt that can heal us. If we can manage to summon up the courage to face our real omissions and failures in life, we can begin to grow. It is the painful truth that makes us free.

Real guilt is inevitable in life. We cannot pass through this life without inflicting injury upon others. One person inevitably prospers at the expense of another. No businessman can be a success without damaging or using others—employees or competitors—in one way or another. And what professional person can say that at least occasionally his mistakes have not damaged his clients? Parents inevitably inflict injury upon their children and damage their trust, confidence and love. In spite of what we believe to be our best intentions, our areas of unconsciousness and our inner darkness cause us to injure those whom we love the most (because they are most vulnerable).

To live, to have experiences, is to incur guilt. This is real guilt. It must be faced, and can be faced without injuring the Center of our being. But the neurotic guilt instilled in us by the negative guilt-producing voice does injure. The trouble is, most of us feel guilty about the wrong things, and fail to feel guilty when the guilt really belongs to us.

Let us take a hypothetical, but realistic example. A woman realizes that she is unhappy with her husband, admits that she has strong urges to leave him, and has fantasies about finding another man. She realizes her husband is both weak and tyrannical at the same time. On the one hand he tries to tyrannize her, putting her down with critical comments, and trying to control and manipulate her by his bad moods. On the other hand, he is also a weak child of a man, whom she recognizes is emotionally dependent on her, and who would, she believes, be unable to get along without her to take care of him and be a scapegoat for him. Other people think they are happily married, but that is because her husband only shows his dark side when they are alone, and also because she feigns happiness in the presence of others. As a result, no one knows that their marriage is a sham, and no one knows how unhappy she really is.

But now her unhappiness has become so great that she is forced to face the fact that she dislikes her husband. Prodded by her unhappiness, she reflects upon the circumstances that led to this unhappy union. Thinking about it honestly, she realizes that she never did love this man. When they first met she was miserably unhappy living at home, but had no way to make her way independently through life. Her husband came along and seemed to offer the way out. He was slightly older than she, had a steady job, and seemed to be a presentable person. And of course he was showing her his "nice" side at that time. So it was not hard for her to persuade herself that this was love, but in her heart she knew then, and realizes now, that she never did love him. He was simply the only way out of her unpleasant situation. So she married, and since she could not admit to herself her real motives for marrying, she pretended for many years, to herself, to him, and to others, that she loved him. She kept this up for a long time, even after he had long since stopped being "nice" to her and had begun to dominate her.

But finally her real feelings could no longer be denied. She became depressed and realized how she really felt about her marriage. Now she knew why she had the powerful urges to leave, and why she had such fantasies about another man who suddenly seemed terribly attractive to her.

So she considered leaving. They had two children, but they

were fairly grown up now. Still, the children *were* there. How would they feel about it? To be sure, they were not overly fond of their father, but he was their father, and he seemed to depend on them, as well as on her, for whatever happiness he got out of life in his egocentric way. Did she have a right to take his children away from him by getting a divorce?

Now the guilt-producing thoughts begin to roll in. The Inner Critic goes to work on her: "You cannot leave. If you do you will be bad. You made a vow when you married him to remain with him always. Now you want to break the vow just to seek your own happiness. You do not care about his happiness or the happiness of your children. You are a selfish woman. If he is not happy with you it is because you have rejected him. You must be kinder to him. Look how you deny him sex! You have no right to do this. You are his wife. If you leave him all your friends and neighbors will know how bad you are, and they will be right. Your husband may even become ill with the shock of it. He could even commit suicide. Remember when he once threatened to kill himself if you ever left him? If he kills himself, *you* are to blame. . . ." On and on the voice goes, and the woman feels she can't leave the marriage; her self-image goes down and down, for by now she is convinced that the voice is right: She is a bad person even to have such thoughts.

Finally in her distress she goes to a counselor and tells her the story. The counselor listens carefully and, without giving direct advice, does point out some other things to her: "Your urge to get away is part of your desire to find your own health. If one person is drowning, does it help if another person tries to save him if the drowning person pulls them both down? If your husband chooses to commit suicide that is between him and God; you cannot take responsibility for it. If others criticize you, that is for you to face. Your real friends will understand. Your children may be shocked if you leave their father, but is that worse than living a sham relationship in front of their eyes? If you

leave you may seem to damage other people, but at least you
will be real. Is it true that you remain with him to protect others
from hurt? Or is it that you lack the courage to take responsibility for your own decision and assume the burden of your own
life? And are you more guilty to leave or to stay? Now your
husband is living with a woman who does not want him. If you
leave he has a chance to find another woman who may want to
be with him. It also gives him a chance to be himself. Do you
remain in the marriage for love, for morality, or because of fear?
Do you refuse to leave because you are so kind and righteous, or
because you are afraid to admit to yourself your awful mistake
in marrying him in the first place and paying the price for it
openly?"

The woman is forced to admit that the counselor has some
points. In fact, she had some of those thoughts herself from time
to time, but hardly dared let herself think them. Still, she wonders, which is her true Conscience? It is not always easy to tell.
But it is clear that her feelings of guilt in the situation are compounded from feelings of false guilt and real guilt. It is also clear
that by staying in the marriage she feels like a coward. And yet,
she cannot so easily rid herself of the belief that the dark side of
her, the shadowy side that demands freedom from the stifling
marriage, must be bad. Would it not make a wreck of everything? If she gave way to it the wreckage of the marriage would
be strewn all over. The lives of the children would be uprooted
(though maybe the change would be for the better), and her
husband's misery would be incalculable (or so she imagines).
But which is worse—her seemingly dark side that would break
up the home, or her cowardly ego that lives a sham life?

Let us take another example. A man is married to an overbearing woman. She wasn't always that way, but the longer they
have been married the more dominating she has become. She
wants her own way and bullies him, and also the children, into
giving in to her. When crossed she goes into a rage, or she pouts

and will not speak to anyone, which makes them feel so uncomfortable that they give in to her. The man likes peace and harmony. He believes it is wrong to fight, and he has seen what a bad effect it apparently has on everyone when he does put up any resistance to her. So for a long time he has bought peace by letting her have her own way. The worse she becomes the "nicer" and more obliging he is.

Soon in the eyes of those who know them he is the good guy and she is the warhorse. Even the children agree that their father is kind. He himself believes that his kindness is a virtue, that he is a loving man, and that his task in life is to hold the family together and produce what peace and kindness there is. Strangely enough, his wife's response to his kindness is to get worse and worse.

Finally one day she becomes even more overbearing than usual; she actually orders him around like a servant. Deep inside of him something snaps. Before he knows what he is doing he shouts an obscenity at her and strikes her in the face. His wife crumples. She falls on the couch sobbing about no one loving her. Instantly her husband falls into a state of painful remorse. "Look at the evil you have done!" his Inner Critic hurls at him. Unable to stand her crying, and riddled with guilt, the husband stifles his anger again. He is all solicitude for her now, full of apologies, begging for forgiveness. For just a moment his wife looks at him appealingly; she actually looks like a woman he could love, but as he becomes more obsequious, she once again becomes tyrannical.

Yet his wife is no longer quite so sure of herself, so she arranges an appointment with their minister. The man goes a bit fearfully, but also with a bit of hope. After all, Pastor Smith is a genial fellow and maybe he can be helpful. Pastor Smith listens attentively as they tell their story—with the woman doing most of the talking. Then he talks to them about God and His love, and he cannot restrain himself from reminding his errant parishioner that it was wrong for him to strike his wife and that he must never do that again.

They both thank Pastor Smith for his help, and before long they are back in the old pattern again, only worse than ever. For whenever he shows the slightest spirit his wife reminds him of the terrible time when he struck her, and what a bad person he is to have done such a thing.

Where is the husband's guilt? Certainly it is—usually—a bad thing to hit other people. Pastor Smith made that clear to him, and his own Inner Critic reminds him of it all the time. Without realizing it, the man has an inner child who remembers a similar incident: There was the time his mother scolded him for something he did not do, and he spoke up defiantly and said bad words to her and she shut him up in his room for two days and would not let anyone in the family speak to him. He concludes that he is a bad person and he must never get angry again.

But he is unhappy, unhappier than he was before. He feels like a caged animal who had a taste of freedom and then was shut up again in a smaller cage than the one he was in before. In his extremity he goes to a friend and tells him his story, but his friend gives him a different point of view. "It must have felt good to tell her off," his friend suggests. "Sounds to me like she deserved to be hit. For once you must have felt like a man."

The husband disagrees vehemently with his friend. "It did no good to talk with him," he thinks to himself. And yet as he goes home certain other thoughts come to him. He remembers that after he hit his wife and she lay there on the couch crying, for one brief moment he felt a flicker of the old love for her that he once had. The thought comes to him: Maybe when you try to appease your wife's anger you are only encouraging her to dominate you. Maybe when you try to be so nice to her when she acts badly you are only cheating her of a chance to come up against someone who will not accept her nastiness, and this denies her a chance to grow and change. You think you are being a loving martyr. Could it be, in fact, that you are a sham when you act like this? Could it be that when you were angry at her you were genuine?

Real guilt and false guilt—they get all mixed up together. The one that poses as the voice of God may actually be the false voice. The other, which sometimes looks like the devil, may actually have behind it the power of the real Center to our personality. How can we tell the difference?

To return to the woman in our first example, no matter what she does guilt will be involved. If she breaks up the marriage she is certain to feel guilt, not just over the distress she is causing others, but also over the fact that her unconsciousness of her motives led her into such a union in the first place. But if she stays in the marriage she is guilty too—guilty of living a false life, and of posing as someone she is not.

The man in our second example also cannot escape guilt. No one can allow himself to be driven to such a deep repression of his anger and emotions that they burst out in phsycial violence without having to assume some guilt. But perhaps his greater guilt lies in having been so "nice," in covering over his cowardice by playing the role of the kind man who is a long-suffering martyr.

Real guilt and false guilt do get mixed together in our minds. Yet clearly the Inner Critic who inspires false guilt in us is to be found, in both of the above examples, on the side of a sham marriage and sham relationship. Though it speaks with authority it develops phony people.

And that is where our egocentricity is in a secret alliance with the false guilt-producing voice. Yes, we complain about the depression that our false guilt inspires in us. Yet the fact is, if we were to cast aside that false guilt we would have to become genuine people. We would have to become strong and psychologically honest with ourselves. We would have to assume our unhappiness as our own problem, and we could not whine about it anymore. The truth is, deep in our hearts, we may prefer the neurotic suffering to the task of having to pull our own oar in life.

What will these two people do? We do not know, of course, for both examples are hypothetical, though the ingredients for both are drawn from real-life stories. There is a good chance that the woman in the first example will stay in her unhappy marriage, and that the man in the second will continue to live the life of a coward under the pose of being long-suffering. They will certainly do so unless they can free themselves of their need to have an outer cause to blame for their inner problems.

In the final analysis, the Inner Critic gets its power from our phony, egocentric egos. But if at last we find the courage to break free of the Inner Critic and the false guilt, we can move away from the confinements of our egocentricity into a more spontaneous life. It is all a great risk, of course. There is no guarantee that in breaking away from the guilt-producing Inner Critic we will wind up on the right side. Maybe, after all, we will just be the terrible person the Inner Critic tells us we will be. Life gives no guarantees, and if God told us exactly what to do, He would only make us more egocentric than ever. No, we act boldly, we take the chance. We weigh all the alternatives. Then at last we act.

Chapter Eight
Indirect Communication

So far we have been discussing direct attempts at communication, but sometimes, as was suggested earlier, communication is undertaken indirectly, even involuntarily. There are various ways this may be done, but in each case it is as if the life within us desperately needs to communicate with others even when we do not consciously want such communication to take place.

One way in which indirect communication may take place is through the body, which sends its own signals even though we may not be aware of them. Examples of body communication include all the psychogenically induced physical symptoms with which a doctor is familiar—the high blood pressure that turns out to be a result of stress or anxiety, the simulated heart attack that turns out to have no organic basis, and a host of other symptoms, from dizziness to headaches, that may have no organic basis.

Body communication also includes so-called body language. As we unconsciously wring or twist our hands we are telegraphing to others a message about our unexpressed anger, frustration, or tension. Our stooped posture or slow, somber way of walking is like a neon light that tells the world about the great psychological burden we are carrying, our despair, or our feeling of spiritual fatigue. The unconscious changes of inflection in our voice often say more than our words about how we are feeling, and people who are sensitive to others respond to voice modulation as well as to words.

Skillful doctors and counselors learn to observe the body movements of their patients. A good physician has her patient under scrutiny from the moment she steps into her office. A therapist may observe the way his client comes up the stairs to meet him; he notices what his client's hands are doing as he talks; he observes the way he walks when he leaves. All of this tells him a great deal about his client's inner state. These body messages can be an open book that can be easily read by those who know the language.

But you do not have to be a doctor or therapist to learn to read these messages. Anyone who is interested in other people, takes the time to be observant, and uses common sense can read the body signals that almost all of us send out. They can tell us a lot, for it is as though a person's body wants someone to know what is going on, even though the person does not speak up about his inner feelings.

Other forms of involuntary communication take place through some kind of unconscious psychological mechanism. One of the most common of these is the so-called slip of the tongue. These occur when we consciously intend to say one thing but say something else instead. We hear some slips of the tongue even as we make them; others are so subtle that we are not aware of them at all, though others hear them clearly. Slips of the tongue can be merely humorous or have a more devastating effect. Such was the case when Mayor Daley of Chicago proclaimed in a public announcement that "the policeman isn't there to create disorder; the policeman is there to preserve disorder."

A good "Christian" woman, who was quite angry at another woman in her parish, once said to me, "I spoke to her *venom*ently." Of course she meant to say "vehemently." Her slip of the tongue betrayed the angry and vindictive feelings she had toward the other woman which she was not able to admit to herself. But indirectly, through the slip of the tongue, the dark feelings succeeded in communicating themselves.

It is not just the conscious ego who wants to communicate; communication is not something we decide to do. It is a necessity urged upon us from within. For this reason, when we fail to communicate on a conscious level, the unconscious may do the job for us.

This frequently occurs, for instance, when we are keeping a personal secret. There is something in us that does not like to keep secrets for any egocentric purpose, and as a result there is a pressure within us to let the secret out. It is especially difficult to keep it from surfacing when the secret concerns or involves the life of someone else. Of course it is a different matter when we are holding confidential information for the sake of others. So the doctor, the priest, or a close friend can safely guard the secrets of his confidants.

But secrets that we hold for our egocentric purposes are not healthy. They become encased in a kind of guilt, and a considerable pressure builds up from within us to betray these secrets to others. Under such circumstances an involuntary, unconscious communication may occur.

An example: One day a mother walks into her daughter's room to change the sheets. Under the pillow she finds a mysterious looking envelope. She thinks to herself, "What is in that envelope is her business; I should not pry." But of course she does, and inside she finds a suspicious looking white powder. She shows it to her husband who takes it to his friend the pharmacist, who identifies it as a dangerous drug. Now the parents know of their daughter's secret use of drugs.

When confronted, their daughter is full of righteous indignation at this invasion of her privacy. "You had no right to look into that envelope," she says angrily. It seems to her an accident that her mother found the envelope, and unjust that she looked into it. But no one leaves such evidence around if there is not a hidden desire that the secret matter be found out. If the young girl were completely honest with herself she would admit that she is relieved the matter has come to light. Of course she won't say so, but she is glad that mother and father are aware of her secret now, for she wanted help with her problem but could not bring herself to ask for it.

Let us take another hypothetical but true-to-life example. It is not unusual for John to look into his wife's purse; he often does so, with her full knowledge, to locate the checkbook so he can pay the bills, or for some other legitimate reason. But one day when he reaches into his wife's purse he discovers strange-looking notes. Naturally he looks at them, and is soon informed of his wife's secret love affair with another man.

We can guess why John's wife left the telltale evidence in just the place where her husband would find it. She was divided within herself about her affair. Part of her *wanted* her secret to be known. Of course she is angry at her husband for invading her privacy, but another part of her is relieved. Now, perhaps something can be settled. At least she will not have to carry around her hidden guilt.

The secret love affair is particularly difficult to keep secret. Our love relationships outside of our marriage, or primary relationship, fairly cry out to be communicated. It takes a surprising amount of energy to keep the secret hidden. If a person has such a secret she has to be thinking all the time or she will betray her love affair to her partner. And sooner or later the unconscious almost always sees to it that she makes a mistake. For the demand from within for communication is stronger than the ego's fear of having the secret come out. In fact, probably in most cases where a secret love affair is going on and the concerned partner does not learn about it, he really does not want to.

When someone is unusually careful to keep a love affair secret, and unusually capable at doing so, the communication may still take place from the unconscious of one person to the unconscious of the other person. In this case, the person who is being betrayed often dreams about the love affair of her partner. It is usually a woman who dreams about her husband's secret love affair, sometimes actually seeing him with the identical woman with whom he is having his secret rendezvous. It is as though communication that should have been taking place consciously between two people has been blocked, and so it goes underground and takes place via the unconscious. Why it should so often be this way is a puzzle. Surely, we think, we should have a choice in the matter. But the purposes of life are stronger than the purposes of the ego, and the purposes of life are seldom served by secrets.

Sometimes direct means of communication seem too risky or too difficult. We want someone to know how we feel, but we cannot bring ourselves to tell him in so many words. Perhaps it is an inhibition that holds us back, or a fear of rejection, or perhaps the person with whom we wish to communicate is a difficult person, prone to take things the wrong way. For whatever reason, it sometimes happens that people deliberately decide to communicate indirectly rather than directly.

John and Mary have had a quarrel. John is now over his anger and is sorry that he said those unkind things to Mary. However, he can't bring himself to apologize. But, quite uncharacteristically, he offers to go to the grocery store for her when she announces that evening that she is tired. If Mary is alert she will recognize that in her husband's unusual behavior he is trying to tell her that he is sorry and wants to make up.

Children may do this too. A little boy has made his mother

angry by his behavior. Later he comes into the house with a little gift for her. He picked the daffodil in the garden and brings it to her as a present. We can only hope that his mother will not be angry again because he has plucked an important flower from the garden without permission. We hope she will recognize in the act that her son wants to be on good terms with her once more.

The language of love is apt to be especially indirect because love is intimate and gets close to the soul, so we often are afraid of its direct expression. In fact, sometimes it is better if love is communicated indirectly rather than directly, and people instinctively recognize this.

A young man sees an especially attractive young woman at school. He longs to approach her and get acquainted but doesn't know how. He is too shy to come up and say, "What is your name?" Besides, he is afraid this might drive her away from him. Because he fears rejection and fears he might win her disfavor by approaching her too directly, he finds an indirect way to communicate his interest. He just "happens" to be outside school when she leaves the school grounds, and just "happens" to fall in with her, saying, "Didn't I see you the other day at the football game?" (knowing full well that he hadn't). The young lady may recognize that the young man is indirectly saying to her, "You are attractive to me. I would like to get better acquainted, but is it possible?"

Men are especially likely to be indirect when they communicate love to a woman, but women can also be indirect in the messages that they give. A woman has been quarreling with her husband because he watches so much football on television on the weekends. Because of this she feels hurt and shut out, and as a result they have had a terrible argument about it. He has tried to make a compromise, and has suggested that after the game they go out to dinner. Haughtily she refuses. Now she decides to change her mind; she decides it is all right for him to watch the football game if it is that important to him. And before the game ends she brings him a cup of coffee. The message is clear: "Let's make up."

It is easy to become disdainful about indirect communication. Often we will find ourselves saying that the other person is a coward, that he should come right out and say what he feels and not beat about the bush. Especially in love matters, a woman may virtually demand that her man tell her what he feels, and be inclined to reject indirect forms of communication. Sometimes it *is* a kind of cowardice, if we can call the fear of rejection cowardice. And sometimes it is a false pride that causes us to communicate indirectly rather than directly. Even then we may wish to accept forms of indirect communication in a good spirit. It is, after all, better than no form of communication at all.

There are occasions when indirect communication is better than direct communication. Matters of the heart are often better expressed in a dim light rather than a glaring one. Subtle feelings call for subtle means of conveying them. In this day and age, when we demand so much openness, and value what we call "being honest," it is easy to forget the subtle language of love. It is like flowers: some do best in the full sun, but others grow better in partial shade.

When all other means of communication have been exhausted, some people will try to communicate with what is known as "acting out." In acting out, a person represents inner feelings by means of his actions. What an observer sees is just the behavior, but underneath the behavior is the person's agenda, his feelings, needs, and thoughts that want to be heard, but have been denied. So he resorts to acting out.

For instance, a married woman has an affair with another man. Curiously, she manages to have her husband find out about it. Perhaps she even boldly tells him herself. He is hurt and angry and naturally accuses her of loving someone else and being unfaithful to him. The truth is that she does not love the man with whom she had the affair; she loves her husband, but he has become so absorbed in his business, so taken over by his own many concerns, so confident that his wife will always be ready and waiting for him, that he has not heard her pleas for more of a share in his life, and more expression of his feelings. Time and again she has tried to bring up matters of their relationship and has been brushed aside. So finally she decides to have an affair, though what she really wants is to get her husband's attention. And she succeeds. She *does* have her husband's attention now, and he is angry, hurt, and involved. The two of them have an angry confrontation. The woman rather relishes it, but she is also fearful lest she has gone too far, and anxious lest she will not be able to get across what it is that she really wants from him.

The possibility that she might not succeed in getting her message across is complicated by two factors. One complication comes from the fact that she herself may not be entirely aware of what she has been up to. Her plot to have the affair in order to get her husband's attention may have been hatched in some dark corner of her being and her motives may not be entirely clear even to her.

A second complication comes because her husband is now terribly upset. His own emotions compel him to give her the attention she wants, but those very emotions are also a barrier to communication; they make it more difficult for him to hear his wife's subtle and tender feelings. The whole matter might not end in understanding at all, but might turn into a bad scene from which the relationship cannot recover. For that is the problem when we use acting out in order to communicate. Such behavior may break up the logjam and get communication going again, but it may also make things worse than they were before.

When we are forced to act out in order to communicate, things are pretty bad. Like the hypothetical girl who wrote the imaginary letter we included in the first chapter, the state of alienation is almost always extreme when acting out is chosen as a means of last resort.

The use of drugs, antisocial behavior, flunking in school—all of these forms of behavior may be indirect attempts to communicate. Suicide attempts sometimes fall into this same category. Many people "try" to commit suicide but do not succeed. What they succeed in doing is attracting a lot of attention to themselves. Family, friends, doctors, perhaps even the police, are summoned, and, for a while at least, the would-be suicide becomes the center of a great deal of energy. Such unsuccessful suicide attempts may be compounded of many factors. There may be a genuine ambivalence about going on with life. Yes, she *wants* to die, and so she takes a lot of pills; but there is the other part of her that does not want to die, so she does not take quite enough to kill herself, or, having taken them, she calls a friend to tell her what she has done. There may also be aggression in it, for suicide attempts can be, at least in part, hostile acts directed against offending persons of personal importance. But the suicide attempt can also be an attempt at communication: "Look at me. See my distress! See how unhappy I am. See how angry I am with you. See how much I want someone to come and help me!"

Again, not all of this is part of a conscious plan on the part of the would-be suicide. When it comes to acting out behavior, the plots are hatched in the shadowy realm between the conscious and unconscious mind. At such a time people are seldom clear about what they are doing and why.

Tom, as we can call him, was divorced and married again to a woman who was also divorced and had three teenage children. Tom and his new wife got along fairly well when they were alone, but not when the children were around. In Tom's view, their mother was too permissive, and he thought the teenage children behaved badly. Time and again Tom tried to get his wife to discipline them more stringently, and sometimes he tried

to exert authority on his own. But his wishes were denied. Their
mother did not share Tom's views about discipline. She did not
want him to take a role in the lives of her beloved children. She
did not believe that what they were doing was so bad and did not
want to change her patterns of relating to them, and the teenage
children definitely did not want their stepfather to assume the
role of a disciplinarian who would impose and enforce certain
rules upon them.

One day the pressure of family life got to him and Tom
went beserk. He was a big, rough kind of man, and when the
dam broke and all his rage came out, it was like the proverbial
bull in a shop of fragile china. Tom heaved furniture around, he
smashed lamps, he threw a chair into the TV set and left it in
pieces on the floor. He hurled the refrigerator to the floor and
everything spilled out of it. The frightened wife and children fled
from the house. It was very dramatic. The police were called and
came to the door, while anxious neighbors hovered around. But
it turns out there is no law against a person's smashing his own
property, and no one had been hurt, so Tom did not go to jail, but
eventually he did go to a counselor.

When Tom told this story there was an interesting nuance
to it: He did not smash everything: some things in the house
were unscathed. It seems that he knew exactly what he was
smashing and every object he smashed had a story to it. When
he broke the TV he thought of all the times he had tried to
enforce some rules about its use, but had been denied. When he
overthrew the refrigerator, he thought of all the times the children had been allowed to raid it even though it spoiled their
dinner. The list went on and on.

Tom smashed things because he was trying to be heard. He
desperately wanted and needed his new family to know how angry and alienated he felt. Other means failing, his shadow personality did the talking for him. He didn't touch anyone; he
didn't hurt a child, but neither did he succeed in communication,

for not long after, this marriage broke up too. Communication by acting out seldom works. Still, other means of communication haven't worked either by the time we have chosen, on some level of our being, to communicate in this way. Beneath it all is our great need: the need to be heard.

Chapter Nine
People *Are* Different

In Chapter One I noted that people are different, and in Chapter Five I mentioned that some people are thinking type people and they may see things differently than feeling type people. I promised to explain what this means, and the time has come to do so. It is a fact that people *are* different, and if we learn to understand this, and see how our friend, husband, wife, or child is a different kind of person than we are, many misunderstandings can be avoided, and our awareness of these differences will be a bridge spanning the gulf between us and others.

There have been various attempts to describe human typological differences, but the most comprehensive is that of C. G. Jung. Although it is not perfect, it is the best there is, and we will use it to help us understand the differences among people and what this means for communication.

It must be understood, however, that this will be only the briefest survey of the vast and rich field of human typology. I hope there will be enough information in this chapter to be of immediate and practical value in learning to communicate, but the person who wants to understand the matter of types more completely must delve into some of the literature in the field. The foundation work for Jung's typology is by Jung himself. His work *Psychological Types* (CW 6) is a rich and brilliant study, but unfortunately it is too complex and unwieldy for most people. The first part of the slim volume entitled *Jung's Typology*, by Marie-Louise von Franz, is clear and much more concise. Another introductory book is by Isabel Briggs Myers, whose volume *Introduction to Type* is highly practical. Isabel Myers is one of the originators of the Myers-Briggs Types Indicator, a simple psychological test that helps people determine their own typology. Some of her research with this test has been summarized in her most recent volume, *Gifts Differing*, a book that includes special information about typology and marriage.[1]

Let us begin with the two basic orientations toward life. Most of us are aware that some people are known as extraverts and some as introverts. What we may not know is that C. G. Jung is the man who perceived that people are fundamentally different in their attitude to life, some of them being involved with and fascinated by the world outside of themselves, and others being involved and drawn to their subjective, inner processes. He called these two orientations to life extraversion and introversion. Actually extraversion and introversion are two poles on a spectrum, and we must imagine the human race sprinkled along the entire length of this spectrum. Thus some people might be described as strongly extraverted and some as strongly introverted, while others fall closer to the middle, and for a few it may be hard to tell which orientation to life is most favored.

The thoughtful philosopher contemplating life, the reflective psychologist peering into the depths of his psyche, the religious contemplative pursuing God in his own quiet way, and

---

[1] Isabel Myers' books, and others as well, can be obtained from the Center for Applications of Psychological Types, Inc., 1441 Northwest Sixth Street, Suite B-400, Gainesville, Florida 32601.

the naturalist rejoicing in her solitary walks among nature might all be examples of introverts. The politician or statesman glorying in the realm of busy human life, the engineer involved with building cities, and the entertainer who is happiest mingling with and pleasing the crowd might be examples of extraverts. Clearly, the basic life orientation of the first group of people seems different from the latter. In the first case it involves a peering inward, in the second a looking outward. This difference is reflected in Greek mythology in the story of Prometheus and his brother Epimetheus—opposite types whose names mean, respectively, forethought and afterthought.

In our culture, extraversion is favored and encouraged, and introversion gets a bad press. In some places introversion is even equated with a kind of sickness. It is sometimes said that it isn't good to be involved with one's self, and the longing of the introvert for times of reflection in which she can withdraw within herself are often looked upon as antisocial, as though she did not like people. But it is not true that extraverts like people more than introverts. Introverts can love people and need people as much as extraverts, only they go about it differently. For instance, friendships among introverts usually involve a relatively few relationships in depth. Extraverts, however, may satisfy their social needs with a broader range of relationships than introverts but with relationships that do not go as deep.

Because extraverts and introverts are so different they see things differently, enjoy different life styles, and have different values. If two people are in a relationship and one is extraverted and one is introverted, a gulf springs up between them. Each may think there is something wrong with the other and this creates an air of criticism and misunderstanding. If this is the case, it helps greatly for the two people to understand their difference in the extraversion-introversion scale. Then they can understand that the other person is not wrong but different, not stubborn in persisting in an erroneous course in life, but genuinely following his own way. By learning to appreciate the point of view of the other person each one becomes a little less one-sided, for each life attitude, if it excludes its opposite, *is* one-sided.

A relationship between an extravert and an introvert is most likely to occur in family life. It is not as likely to happen between friends because we are inclined to pick friends from among persons of our own type. (An extravert and an introvert may be friendly, but are not likely to become close friends; their preferences in life are too different.) But an introverted man may marry an extraverted woman, or the other way around. Then a collision between their different orientations is unavoidable. Or two introverted parents may have an extraverted child, or extraverted parents may have an introverted child. There may then be difficulty on the parents' part in understanding this particular child who seems to be so different, and whose difference is readily misinterpreted as aberrant, undesirable, or willfully stubborn behavior. Communication may then quickly break down unless the parents understand that their child is not wrong, just different.

In addition to the basic life orientations, there are also, according to Jung, four psychological functions. He calls these functions thinking, feeling, sensation and intuition. By function Jung means a certain form of psychological activity or functioning that tends to remain the same even under different circumstances, and which the ego can utilize and develop in order to approach life and cope with problems and difficulties.

Thinking and feeling are termed the rational functions because they enable us to arrive at conclusions. They are related in such a way that the development of one function is done at the expense of the other. Thus we tend to develop thinking at the expense of feeling, and vice versa.

Sensation and intuition are called the irrational functions

because they are concerned with the gathering of information.
They also tend to be mutually exclusive of each other. Thus we
can diagram the four functions as follows:

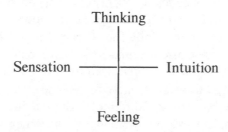

The idea is that in their development each person utilizes
and develops one of these four functions. This becomes the primary function and gives that person his primary typology. The
function that is developed is usually the easiest for that person to
use and becomes the most effective tool for that particular person's ego. (It is usually a matter of heredity.) Depending on
which is the most developed function, we can speak of a thinking
type of person, a feeling type, an intuitive type or a sensation
type.

The thinking type approaches life with an analytical, logi-
cal approach. A person who uses this function attempts to ana-
lyze situations and arrive at conclusions based upon the logic of
a situation as illuminated by his powers of discrimination and
conceptualization. In our particular culture thinking types are
rewarded. Our educational system favors the thinking type, and
thinking types may well find their money earning potential is
greater than other types of people, other things being equal.

The feeling function approaches life in order to evaluate it;
it is the valuing function. A person who uses this function arrives
at conclusions also, like the thinking type, but his conclusions
concern matters of value. "This is good, this is bad, that is terrible, this is desirable . . ." are the conclusions of the feeling type

of person. This type is often at a disadvantage because we live in a culture that is not concerned with values but with power.

The sensation type is a gatherer of information. The person with this function is aware of the outer world. This is the person who notices things, who can tell you the color of the sofa in the living room of the friend whose house she was in last night. The sensation function is interested in the outer world of tangible facts and comes to conclusions through the senses of the body.

The intuitive type also gathers information but gains this information through intuition, "the eyes of the soul." The intuitive person perceives possibilities, sees things that do not yet exist but might exist, and also (if introverted) can see the world of the psyche, the mysterious inner world with its shadows and images that are not perceivable through the bodily senses but can be seen intuitively.

I mentioned that the intuitive can see into the psyche if introverted. This points out that each psychological function is attached to a person with either an extraverted or introverted psychological orientation. The psychological orientation determines the focus of the psychological function. Thus an extraverted thinking type of person may turn her analytical functions to the economic system of the nation and become an important economist. The introverted thinking person, on the other hand, might become a research chemist working in relative isolation in a laboratory. An extraverted feeling type might become a social reformer, involved in social concerns and values, or an outgoing parish priest or minister; an introverted feeling type might be more concerned with the development of family life, or might become a psychotherapist. An extraverted sensation type might become a biologist, enthralled and attentive to a world of facts, but an introverted sensation type might become an accountant, engrossed in the figures of financial reports. An extraverted intuitive might become a talented developer, a person who "sees" how a dead and dying city could be rebuilt, or the possibilities for developing some unused land, while an intraverted intuitive might become a poet or a historian.

To take some historical examples, Albert Einstein was probably an introverted intuitive or thinking type. Jung was said to be an introverted thinking type, but Freud, so Jung thought, was a different type than he was, and this is one reason they disagreed. I suspect that Charles Darwin was an extraverted sensation type; he went around the world noticing things others had overlooked, seeing facts that had been passed over. A man like Abraham Lincoln, however, shows evidence of considerable development in all four functions, which is one reason why we look back upon him as a man who was unusually complete in his personality.

We have spoken of the primary function, but what of the other three functions? They too play their part. Two of the other functions prove to be capable of development along with the primary function. Thus a thinking type of person may also develop intuition or sensation as an auxiliary function. We then speak of an extraverted (or introverted) thinking-sensation or thinking-intuitive type. But the fourth function, which in practice seems always to be the opposite of the primary function, lags behind. It never does seem to develop to the point where the ego can consciously will, direct, or use it. Its role in individuation, the process of becoming whole, is crucial, but that lies beyond the scope of this book. For our present purposes it is enough for us to know that each of us has a certain orientation toward life and utilizes certain of four possible psychological functions, and this may make us a fundamentally different type of person than our friend, parent, wife, husband, employer, or employee with whom we must communicate.

If we do not understand our differences there may be endless difficulties in communication, as I have pointed out, because the two people see things from such a different standpoint. Take political matters, for instance. A thinking type may argue:

"Communism is a menace. Therefore wherever it appears, it must be opposed, by force if necessary." A feeling type person, thinking of the horrors of war, may say, "War is terrible. Whatever happens we must try to avoid it." Each person has points in his favor. Each person's point of view is also limited. Each person may conclude that the other person is "heartless" or "sentimental" simply because neither understands that the other person is speaking from a different standpoint.

Of course a whole or complete point of view would have to see a given situation from the perspective of all four functions. This is an ideal that is hardly likely, but it is possible for a person to broaden her original one-sided standpoint by learning to appreciate the standpoint of other people who are psychologically different. One valuable result of learning to relate to other people is that we learn to appreciate the other person's standpoint as well as our own. In this way we develop a broader personality.

If a thinking type of man marries a feeling type of woman, for instance, they may quarrel bitterly, until they decide that they *are* different and that it is better to understand that fact and appreciate the other person's differences. If, then, the thinking type of man begins to understand his wife, he incorporates some of her feeling perspective into himself, and vice versa. In this way each person becomes less one-sided and more complete.

The theory of the functions has many applications, but perhaps it is especially important for a marriage. Isabel Briggs Myers, in her book already mentioned, devotes an entire chapter to "Type and Marriage." To begin with, she notes that men and women are likely to marry persons of roughly the same type as themselves. And after administering the Myers-Briggs Personality Inventory Test to many hundreds of couples, she concludes that there are more similarities than differences among married couples.

Nevertheless, men and women of opposite types *do* marry. Such marriages, she points out, present special difficulties in communication, but also offer special possibilities for the development of each partner if the differences are recognized and respected.

Marriage counselors often find it helpful to give the Myers-Briggs Type Indicator Test, or a comparable test such as the Gray-Wheelwrights Jungian Type Survey, to their clients as a basis for future discussion. Individuals often also profit from taking these tests in order to help them define for themselves their basic typology. Any trained psychologist should be able to administer the tests, which are simple to take and, since they do not diagnose pathology, are non-threatening in nature. Of course, like any human instrument, the type tests are not infallible, nor can they accurately describe all the intricacies of any individual personality, but they give us a basic grasp of our fundamental psychological approach to life.

Whether we take tests or not, the important fact for each of us to remember is that we *are* different from each other. In the last analysis, good communication between people may depend on the ability of one person to respect the right of another person to be himself. This is one of the things that love is all about, and love is the great facilitator of communication between fellow human beings.